# A Touch of Style

## Sewing Simple, Inventive Clothes
## by Pieke Stuvel

PENGUIN BOOKS

Penguin Books Ltd, Harmondsworth,
Middlesex, England
Penguin Books, 625 Madison Avenue,
New York, New York 10022, U.S.A.
Penguin Books Australia Ltd, Ringwood,
Victoria, Australia
Penguin Books Canada Limited, 2801 John Street,
Markham, Ontario, Canada L3R 1B4
Penguin Books (N.Z.) Ltd, 182–190 Wairau Road,
Auckland 10, New Zealand

First published in the Netherlands under the title
'N Tik van de mode: Zelfmaakmode voor vrouwen die
hun eigen gang gaan by Uitgeverij Bert Bakker 1978
This English translation first published in the United
States of America by Penguin Books 1981

LIBRARY OF CONGRESS CATALOGING IN PUBLICATION DATA
Stuvel, Pieke.
  A touch of style.
  Translation of 'n Tik van de mode.
  1. Dressmaking.  2. Sewing.  I. Title.
TT515.S86313  646'.34  80-24729
ISBN 0 14 046.482 4

Printed in the United States of America by
Capital City Press, Montpelier, Vermont
Set in CRT Roma

# CONTENTS

For Martijn

# FOREWORD

7

Fashion and change are two concepts that are entirely interrelated—there is nothing that changes the way fashion does. But fortunately the day is past when designers could dictate to women. Never before has fashion been so versatile or has such a multiplicity of styles and shapes been presented. This is something to be glad about, because the wider the choice, the greater the likelihood of finding something that fits one's individual figure and character.

The birth of a new style is often a joyous moment—the "ideal" line is always different and there is continuous movement—but a new style does not mean that everything preceding it has suddenly become worthless. A quality article of clothing is of lasting value and, used in a different manner, can often be adapted to the new spirit of the times. Personally I prefer an individualistic style which incorporates the old as well as the new.

The clothing here is mostly simple and reasonably easy to make—and always open to adaptation in different ways. And because we are dealing with clothes that you make yourself, the style can always be personalized by application of your own ideas.

The sizes run from 10 through 16. The patterns are so simple that a reduction to size 8 or an enlargement to size 18 or 20 is easily accomplished.

**—Pieke Stuvel**

# SIZE TABLE

| | Bust | Waist | Hips |
|---|---|---|---|
| Size 10 | 32½ inches (81¼ cm) | 25 inches (62½ cm) | 34½ inches (87 cm) |
| Size 12 | 34 inches (85 cm) | 26½ inches (66¼ cm) | 36 inches (90 cm) |
| Size 14 | 36 inches (90 cm) | 28 inches (70 cm) | 38 inches (95 cm) |
| Size 16 | 38 inches (95 cm) | 30 inches (75 cm) | 40 inches (100 cm) |

♥ = easy

♥ ♥ = moderately difficult

♥ ♥ ♥ = difficult

## Note

1. Most patterns are drawn in one or two sizes; if the desired size is not indicated, it's fairly simple to enlarge or reduce. The accompanying text will tell you how.
2. Always check your own measurements first.
3. Patterns are always drawn without seam or hem allowances. So cut *at least* ⅝ inch (1½ cm) extra for the seams and 2 to 3 inches (5 to 7½ cm) for the hems.
4. Once the garment has been sewn and is ready to be tried on, always iron the seam edges flat first to get a better sense of the final fit.

# Flounced and Gathered skirt on a wide waistband size 12 ♥ ♥

**I** = waistband front
**II** = waist band back
**III** = gathered skirt front & back
**IV** = top section flounced skirt
**V** = bottom section flounced skirt
**VI** = belt

## I
3/8
2
7 1/2
7 1/2
center fr. fold.
side seam
3/8
8 3/4

## II
1 1/8
2
7 1/2
6 3/4
center b. f. f.
side seam
3/8
8 3/4

## III
14 1/2
gather
3/8
25
25
center front center back — fabric fold.
— side seam.
— bottom —
15 1/2

## IV
19 1/2
gather
9 1/2
C.B. + C.F. FR
sideseam
21

## VI
1 1/8
26 1/2
3/4
3/4

for enlarging and/or Reducing see text.

## V
39
gather
15 1/2
center fr. center back. fabric fold
sideseam
40 1/4

# SKIRTS

A gathered or flounced skirt, both sewn to the same smooth waistband. Gathering is a precise task and demands patience in order to assure that the gathers are evenly divided and sewn straight. For that reason, the skirts at the left of the illustration are easier to make.

## VARIATIONS

You can make the waistband and the rest of the skirt from the same material, but you can also experiment with different colors and/or prints. The skirt on the left can be made long, knee length, or shorter, and with the wide seams sewn to the hemline or with slits. The length on the pattern for both skirts comes to about midcalf.

## FABRIC REQUIRED

Left skirt at calf length—2¼ yards (2 m), 36 inches or 45 inches (90 cm or 115 cm) wide; or 1⅔ yards (1½ m), 54 inches (135 cm) wide.
Flounced skirt at calf length—3⅞ yards (3½ m), 36 inches (90 cm) wide; or 3 yards (2¾ m), 45 inches (115 cm) or 54 inches (135 cm) wide.

## ENLARGING OR REDUCING THE PATTERN

For each size change, add or subtract ½ inch (1¼ cm) at all side seams, so that for size 14 the bottom of the waistband is 9¼ inches (23¼ cm) and for size 16, 9¾ inches (24¼ cm), etc. The length of the waistband is altered by ¼ inch (⅝ cm) per change in size—enlarged or reduced.

## CUTTING

Lay the pattern pieces with the "fabric fold" along the folded edge of the doubled-over material. Cut the bottom part of the gathered skirt (III) and the strips for the flounced skirt (IV and V) twice from the doubled-over fabric. Cut ⅝ inch (1½ cm) extra along all sides for a seam allowance, and about 2½ inches (6¼ cm) extra at the bottom of the skirt for a hem. Snip a small notch in the center bottom of the waistband pieces, at fold, at center top of pattern pieces III and V, and at center top and bottom of pattern piece IV, as an indication of where they are to be joined.

## SEWING

**Gathered Skirt** Gather the tops of the two pattern pieces (III) into 17 inches (43 cm) each—for size 12 = bottom of waistband at the hips. Adjust the gathers evenly. Baste one piece to the front piece of the waistband and the other to the back piece. Make sure that the gathers lie smoothly. The center of the waistband must coincide exactly with the center of the skirt (see small notch). Stitch together carefully, then press seam edges flat, toward waist. Pin the side seams together, matching up the pieces accurately. At the top of the left side seam, leave a 7-inch (18-cm) opening for the zipper. Press the seams open; sew the zipper in by hand or machine. Work the zipper extension into the waistband at the waist, leaving 1 inch (2½ cm) open where a snap fastener, small hook, or button and buttonhole will be placed. Fold under the top of the waistband ¼ inch (⅝ cm), press; fold under again ¼ inch (⅝ cm), easing ends of the zipper into fold. Stitch down. Attach small hook and eye to top of waistband. Turn up the hem and stitch.

**Flounced Skirt** Gather the top of the middle pieces, front and back, into 17 inches (43 cm)—for size 12 = bottom of the waistband at the hips. Adjust the gathers evenly. Baste one piece to the waistband front and one to the waistband back, matching notches. Sew, making sure that the gathers lie smoothly. Gather the top of each bottom strip into 42 inches (106 cm), and attach one to each of the middle strips. Pin the front to the back, matching up the pieces accurately, front and back. Stitch the side seams, leaving open 7 inches (18 cm) at the upper left side for the zipper, which is sewn in by hand or machine.

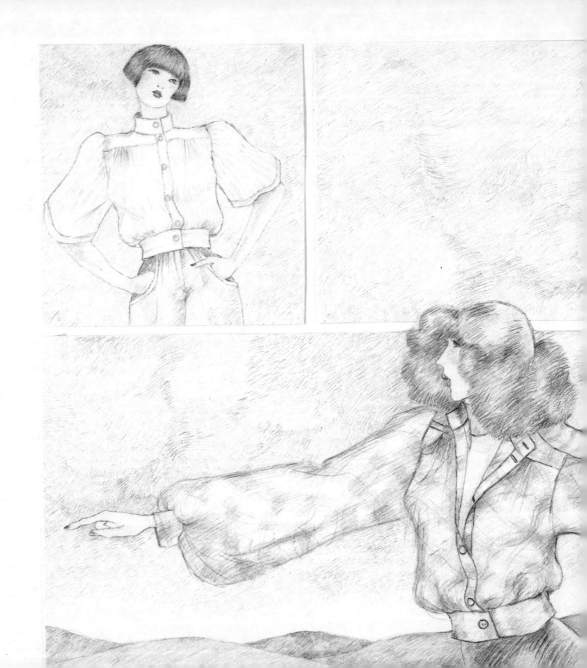

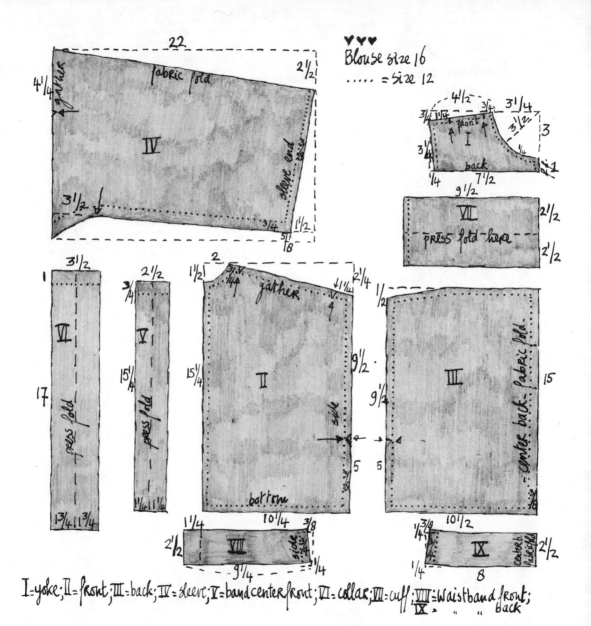

♥ ♥ ♥
Blouse size 16
..... = size 12

22
fabric fold
2½
4¼ gather
IV
3½
¾
1½
5/8
sleeve end

4½
3/4 1¼ 3/4 3¼
front
3½ 3
I
3½ back 1/4
3/8 ft. 1
¼ 7½

9½
VII
2½
PRESS fold here
2½

3½
1
VI
17
press fold
1¾ 1¾

2½
¾
V
15¼
press fold
1¼ 1¼

2
1½ 3½V 2¼
¼
gather 1¼
15¼
II
9½
side
bottom
5
3/16

½
III
center back - fabric fold
9½
9½
15
5
3/16

1¼ 10¼ 3/8
2½ VIII side ¼
¼
9¼

3/8 10½
3/8
¼ IX center b. / lacheld
1¼ 8 2½

I = yoke; II = front; III = back; IV = sleeve; V = band center front; VI = collar; VII = cuff; VIII = waistband front; IX = " " back

# SHORT BLOUSE

A blouse with a mandarin collar and a wide waist-band.

## VARIATIONS
Short or long sleeves, with or without cuffs.

## FABRIC REQUIRED
3 yards (2¾ m), 36 inches (90 cm) wide; or 2¼ yards (2 m), 45 inches (115 cm) or 54 inches (135 cm) wide. Enlarging or reducing the pattern: the pattern is drawn for size 16. The dotted line is size 12. Size 14 lies exactly halfway between these two lines.

## CUTTING
Lay the pattern pieces with the "fabric fold" along the folded edge of the doubled-over material. Cut front and back waistband pieces, the center front band, and the cuff twice from the doubled-over material. Add ⅝ inch (1½ cm) for the seams.

## SEWING
Gather in the two blouse front pieces between the arrows, to 2½ inches (6¼ cm) each. Gather in the top of the blouse back to 15 inches (37½ cm), and pin it to the yoke back, adjusting the gathers evenly, and stitch fast. Pin and stitch the blouse fronts to the yoke front. The gathered area of each blouse front should fall between the arrows at the yoke front. Gather in the sleeve sections between the arrows to 5¼ inches (13½ cm). Stitch the underarm seams of the sleeves. Stitch the side seams of the blouse up to the arrow. Press the seam edges open. Pin and baste the sleeves in place; sew them. Reinforce with an extra line of stitching at the armpits; snip into the seam edges to ease.

Press a thin iron-on strip to the wrong side of the center front band, collar, cuffs, and waistband. Pin and stitch the center front band with the right side against the right side of the blouse front (once on the left, once on the right). Press the seam to the inside, then press the band back along the center line. Hand stitch the center front band to the inside of the blouse. Sew the collar to the blouse in the same manner—do not forget to notch the seam edges at the curve. Stitch the side seams of the waistband together and press the seam edges flat.

Gather in the bottom of each blouse front to 8 inches (20 cm)—without gathering the center front band—and gather the bottom of the blouse back into 16 inches (40 cm). Pin and sew the waistband to the blouse. The blouse seams must align exactly with the waistband seams. Press the seam edges downward. Now pin the waistband lining to the attached waistband, right sides together, and stitch along the outer edges. Trim the seam edge corners, turn right side out, flatten, and press. Sew the waistband lining to the inside of the blouse by hand. Make buttonholes and sew on buttons. Gather the sleeve ends in to 9½ inches (24 cm), dividing gathers evenly, and pin and baste on the cuff, right sides together. Stitch securely, press the seam to the inside, and fold back the cuff to the inside along its center line. Sew the cuff to the inside of the sleeve by hand, then press.

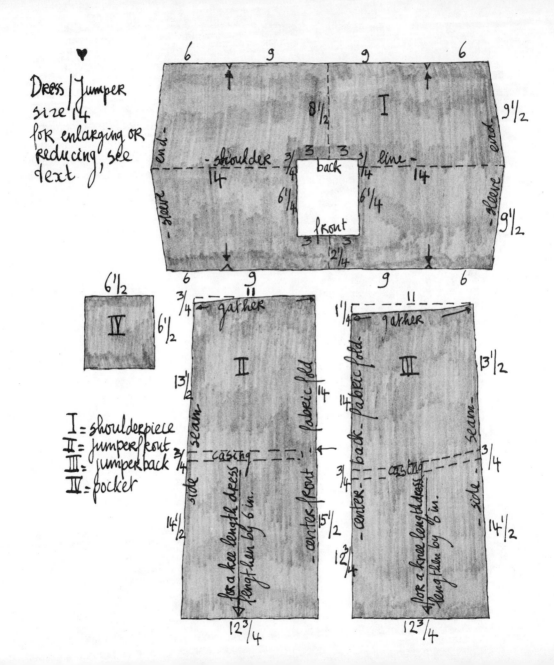

Dress/Jumper
size 14
for enlarging or
reducing, see
text

I = shoulderpiece
II = jumperfront
III = jumperback
IV = pocket

The dress/jumper is gathered onto a single shoulder piece. Worn without a belt, it makes an excellent maternity dress. It is inadvisable to choose a fabric that is too stiff. The softer the material, the more attractive the fall of the garment when worn.

## VARIATIONS
The choice of fabric determines the character of the garment—for example, a cotton for spring and summer, a light wool fabric for autumn and winter. The sleeves can be long or short, and cuffs may be added. Minus pockets and with a casing and belt at the hips, it becomes a blousy short dress that can be worn as a mini-dress or in combination with tight pants.

## FABRIC REQUIRED
For a knee-length dress, 3 yards ($2\frac{3}{4}$ m), 36 inches (90 cm) or 45 inches (115 cm) wide; or $1\frac{2}{3}$ yards ($1\frac{1}{2}$ m), 54 inches (135 cm) wide.

## ENLARGING OR REDUCING PATTERN
For each change in size, enlarge or reduce the shoulder piece by $\frac{1}{2}$ inch ($1\frac{1}{4}$ cm) all around. The arrow marks, between which the gathered dress section is attached, should be moved $\frac{1}{2}$ inch ($1\frac{1}{4}$ cm) outward to enlarge or $\frac{1}{2}$ inch ($1\frac{1}{4}$ cm) inward to reduce, per size change. The neckline is altered $\frac{1}{4}$ inch ($\frac{5}{8}$ cm) per size change all around in enlargement or reduction. The side seams of the dress section are moved $\frac{1}{2}$ inch ($1\frac{1}{4}$ cm) inward or outward per size change.

## CUTTING
Lay the pattern pieces with the "fabric fold" along the folded edge of the doubled-over cloth. Cut $\frac{5}{8}$ inch ($1\frac{1}{2}$ cm) extra on all sides for the seams, and $2\frac{1}{2}$ inches ($6\frac{1}{4}$ cm) extra at the bottom for the hem. For long sleeves, extend the pattern by 12 inches (30 cm). Cut out the pocket 4 times, or cut twice and then twice again for a lining fabric. For a dress with belt casing, cut a strip of material measuring 88 inches (220 cm) by 2 inches (5 cm), and for the belt a strip 60 inches (150 cm) long by 2 inches (5 cm) wide.

## SEWING
Gather in the tops of pattern pieces II and III to 19 inches (48 cm) each for size 14. Adjust the gathers evenly, then pin and baste to the shoulder piece between the arrows. Stitch, then press the seam edges flat and upward. Sew a straight or decorative line of stitching on the right side $\frac{3}{8}$ inch ($\frac{3}{4}$ cm) from the seam. Pin and then sew the underarm seam. Reinforce at the armpit with an extra line of stitching and snip the seam edges almost into the stitching. Press the seam edges open. Trim the neckline with a piece of overlay or piping, cut on the bias. Stitch the pockets, right sides together, leaving an opening. Snip notches in the seam edges, turn right side out, flatten, and press. Then pin on and sew to the dress. Hem the sleeve ends and the hemline of the dress.

**Dress with Belt Casing** Pin, then stitch the casing to the right side of the dress as indicated on the pattern. Allow an opening of about $2\frac{1}{2}$ inches ($6\frac{1}{4}$ cm) at the center front, turning under the raw edges. Make the belt $\frac{1}{2}$ inch ($1\frac{1}{4}$ cm) wide and draw it through the casing.

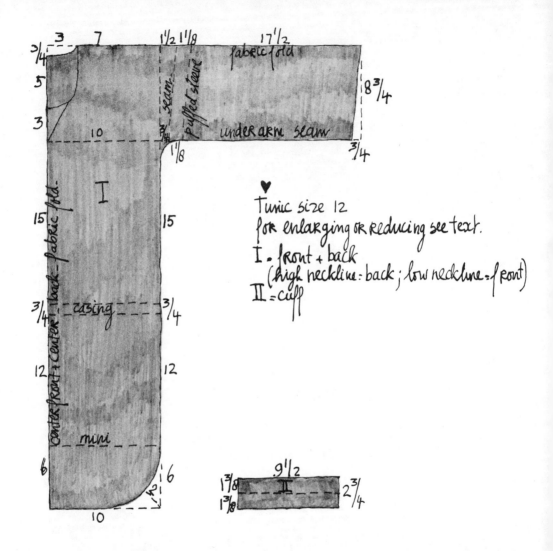

3/4  3  7  1 1/2  1 1/8  17 1/2  fabric fold

5

3  10  8 3/4

3/4
1 1/8  underarm seam  3/4

seam

puffed sleeve

I

15  15

3/4  casing  3/4

center front + center back - fabric fold

12  12

mini

6  6

10

♥
Tunic size 12
for enlarging or reducing see text.
I = front + back
  (high neckline = back; low neckline = front)
II = cuff

9 1/2
1 3/8  II  2 3/4
1 3/8

# TUNIC

It can be worn as a short dress or as a tunic/blouse.

## VARIATIONS

Long sleeves with or without cuffs, short puffed sleeves, closed side seams or with slits. Satin or cotton with stitched-on shoulder patches in a contrasting color.

## FABRIC REQUIRED

**For an above-the-knee dress** $3\frac{2}{3}$ yards ($3\frac{3}{10}$ m), 36 inches (90 cm) wide; or $2\frac{1}{2}$ yards ($2\frac{3}{10}$ m), 54 inches (135 cm) wide.
**For a mini-dress with puffed sleeves** $2\frac{1}{8}$ yards ($1\frac{9}{10}$ m), 36 inches (90 cm) wide.

## ENLARGING OR REDUCING PATTERN

For each change in size, add or subtract $\frac{1}{2}$ inches ($1\frac{1}{4}$ cm) at the underarm and side seams. Lengthen or shorten the sleeve length by $\frac{1}{4}$ inch ($\frac{5}{8}$ cm) per size change. The casing either adds $\frac{1}{4}$ inch ($\frac{5}{8}$ cm) per size change to enlarge or drops $\frac{1}{4}$ inch ($\frac{5}{8}$ cm). The neckline is altered by $\frac{1}{4}$ inch ($\frac{5}{8}$ cm) per size change, either larger or smaller.

## CUTTING

Fold the material twice, first along the width, then the length. Lay the pattern pieces with the "fabric fold" along the folded edges and cut out, allowing $\frac{5}{8}$ inch ($1\frac{1}{2}$ cm) extra for the seams and $2\frac{1}{2}$ inches ($6\frac{1}{4}$ cm) extra at the bottom for the hem.
**Note** Fabrics with an obvious one-way design are not suggested with this pattern, due to the double folding for cutting. For the casing, cut a strip of material 45 inches (115 cm) long by $1\frac{1}{2}$ inches ($3\frac{3}{4}$ cm) wide; for the belt, a strip 60 inches (150 cm) long by $1\frac{1}{2}$ inches ($3\frac{3}{4}$ cm) wide. The dress at the far left of the preceding pages is bound in trim—either buy bias-cut satin binding $5\frac{1}{2}$ yards (5 m) or cut your own trim on the bias, about $1\frac{1}{2}$ inches ($3\frac{3}{4}$ cm) wide. On the others, only the neckline is bound—for that, cut a bias strip 25 inches ($62\frac{1}{2}$ cm) long and $1\frac{1}{2}$ inches ($3\frac{3}{4}$ cm) wide. The trim

at the armhole can be cut straight in 2 pieces 20 inches (50 cm) by $1\frac{1}{4}$ inches (3 cm). For the dress at the far right, also cut a V-shaped strip for the neck [see pattern], the rectangular shoulder patches of 2 pieces 10 inches (25 cm) by 4 inches (10 cm), and the two strips to stitch to the sleeve hems measuring $17\frac{1}{2}$ inches (44 cm) by $4\frac{3}{4}$ inches (12 cm).

## SEWING

Pin and sew the sleeves to the tunic body. Press the seam edges open. Sew a decorative strip about $\frac{1}{2}$ inch ($1\frac{1}{4}$ cm) wide over this seam on the right side. Pin and sew together the side seam and underarm seam in one continuous line. Be careful that the ends of the decorative strip meet each other precisely. Reinforce the armpit with an extra line of stitching, and then snip the seam edges close to the stitching. Pin and sew the belt casing at the indicated place, allowing a 2-inch (5-cm) opening at the center front. Make a belt about $\frac{1}{2}$ inch ($1\frac{1}{4}$ cm) wide and draw it through the casing.
**Model with slits** Evenly round the bottom edges at hemline [see pattern] and measure. Trim the bottom with bias-cut strips. Gather the sleeve ends in to $9\frac{1}{2}$ inches (24 cm). Stitch the cuff seams together. Attach the cuffs, right sides together, turn under, and hand stitch to the inside of the sleeve.
**Dress with shoulder patches** Sew on the shoulder patches, as indicated, then sew the trim along the sleeve insert. Sew the V-patch at the neck, then trim around the neck. Measure the sleeve length, and pin on the strip of trimming 3 inches ($7\frac{1}{2}$ cm) from the desired sleeve hem. Turn overlap back and in, sewing it by hand to the wrong side of the sleeve.
**Mini-dress with puffed sleeves** Cut the pattern at the indicated length. Gather the sleeve end in to the measurement of your upper arm plus $\frac{5}{8}$ inch ($1\frac{1}{2}$ cm) extra width. Cut cuffs 4 inches (10 cm) wide and attach them in the same manner as the cuffs on the long-sleeved tunic. Side seams can either be sewn completely or partially.

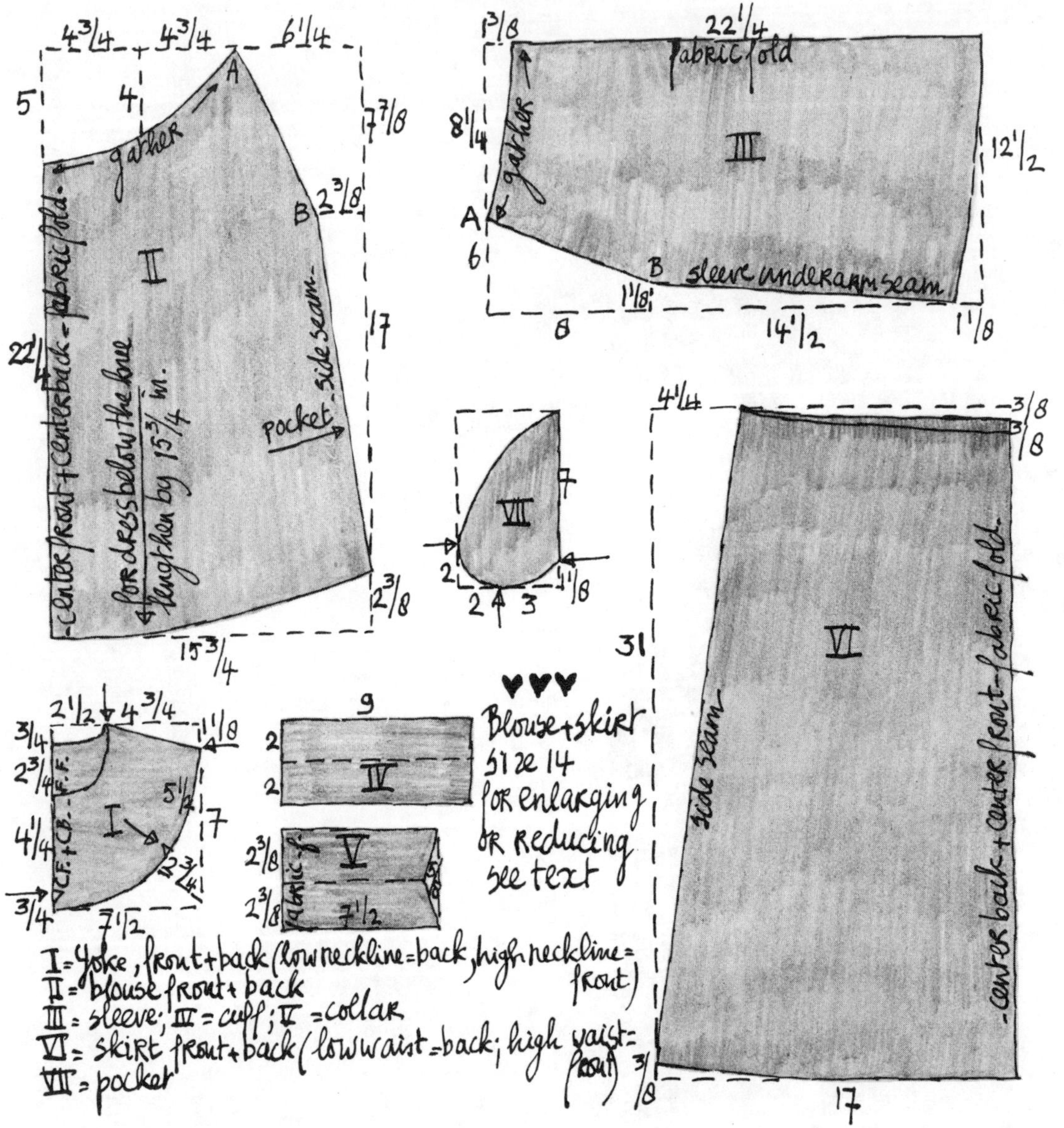

4 3/4
4 3/4
6 1/4
5
4
A
7 7/8
gather
center front + center back – fabric fold.
B
2 3/8
I̲I̲
22 1/4
for dress below the knee lengthen by 15 3/4 in.
side seam.
17
pocket
2 3/8
15 3/4
1 3/8
22 1/4
fabric fold
8 1/4
gather
I̲I̲I̲
12 1/2
A
6
B
sleeve underarm seam
1 1/8
8
14 1/2
1 1/8
7
VII
2
2
3
1 1/8
4 1/4
3/8
3/8
31
V̲I̲
side seam
center back + center front – fabric fold.
3/8
17
2 1/2
4 3/4
1 1/8
3/4
2 3/4
C.F.
5 1/2
I
7
4 1/4
C.F. + C.B.
2 3/4
3/4
7 1/2
9
2
I̲V̲
2
2 3/8
V̲
fabric f.
2 3/8
7 1/2
5/8
♥♥♥
Blouse + skirt
size 14
for enlarging
or reducing
see text
I = Yoke, front + back (low neckline = back, high neckline = front)
II = blouse front + back
III = sleeve; IV = cuff; V = collar
VI = skirt front + back (low waist = back; high waist = front)
VII = pocket

# LOOSE BLOUSE AND SKIRT OR DRESS

A loose blouse that can be lengthened into a dress with pockets in the side seams, made of a soft flowing fabric, and used as a party dress and/or a maternity dress.

## VARIATIONS

Make the yoke the same fabric as the dress, or use a contrasting color or design—leave plain or decorate with appliqués cut from the material.

## FABRIC REQUIRED

**Blouse** 3¾ yards (3½ m), 36 inches (90 cm) wide; or 3⅓ yards (3 m), 45 inches (115 cm) wide.
**Skirt** 1⅞ yards (1¾ m), 36 inches (90 cm) or 45 inches (115 cm) wide.
**Long dress** 5 yards (4½ m), 36 inches (90 cm) wide; or 4⅓ yards (4 m), 45 inches (115 cm) wide.

## ENLARGING OR REDUCING THE PATTERN

For each change in size, add (enlarge) or subtract (reduce) ½ inch (1¼ cm) along the side seams of the front and back pieces. Do the same at the underarm seam of the sleeve and the side seam of the skirt. Either add or subtract ¼ inch (⅝ cm) at bottom edge of the yoke. The neckline is enlarged or reduced by ¼ inch (⅝ cm) per size change. After enlarging or reducing the neckline, measure the neck width and adjust the collar length accordingly.

## CUTTING

Lay the pattern pieces with the "fabric fold" along the folded edge of the doubled-over material. Cut out pattern pieces I, II, III, IV, VI, and VII twice, and pattern piece V once. Cut out pattern piece I once with a high neckline and once with a low neckline. For the gathered skirt, cut the front with a high waistline and the back with a low waistline. Allow ⅝ inch (1½ cm) extra at the seams and 2½ inches (6¼ cm) extra at the bottom for the hem.

## SEWING

Match up and pin together the sections from A to B on the blouse front with the A to B section of the sleeve. Repeat with the sleeve back and blouse back sections. Sew together and press seam edges flat. At the center front of the yoke, cut a straight slit 4½ inches (11 cm), then bind around the neck and opening with edging or a piece of overlay. Stitch the shoulder seams of the yoke to each other, front and back, and press the seam edges flat. Gather the top edges of the blouse front and back into 11 inches (28 cm). Adjust the gathers evenly. Now pin and baste the dress to the yoke—the seam joining the sleeves and the blouse front and back must meet the arrow mark on the yoke. Pin together and sew the underarm and side seams. Reinforce the armpit with an extra line of stitching, and cut into the seam edges almost to the stitching. Gather the sleeve ends in to 9 inches (23 cm), then sew the cuff to the sleeve, right sides facing. Turn the cuff back and sew to the sleeve from the inside by hand.

**Long dress with pockets** Sew on the pockets, two on each dress front and two on each back, matching the arrows, and press the seam edges flat. When stitching the side seams, the pockets will then be sewn in as well. Make slits at sides if desired. The yoke, collar, center slit cut at the neck front, cuffs, and seams can be trimmed or left plain. Pin the collar to the yoke, right sides together, and stitch securely. Press the seam edges upward and sew the collar to the inside of the dress by hand. A button and button-loop can be made at the front to close.

**Skirt** Sew the side seams, leaving partly open for slits if desired. If using a cord to gather in the waist, make a buttonhole at the center front 1¼ inches (3 cm) from the top through which the cord can be drawn. At the top, make a rolled hem of ⅝ inch (1½ cm) and draw the cord or an elastic through it. If using elastic, draw it through an opening in the side seam.

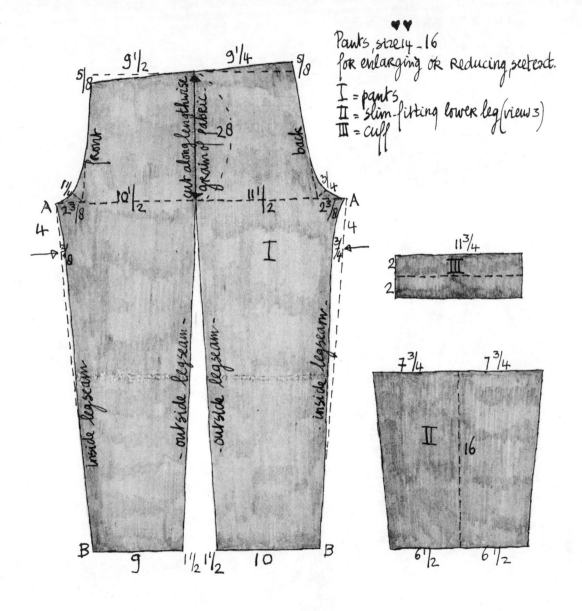

♥ ♥

Pants, size 14-16
for enlarging or reducing, see text.

I = pants
II = slim-fitting lower leg (view 3)
III = cuff

# DRAWSTRING PANTS

A very loose pair of pants that are like pajama bottoms—roomy at the waist and hips and tapering at the bottom. The pants are fastened with a cord drawn through a casing. For those accustomed to tighter pants, these will take some getting used to, but they are very comfortable, do not pull anywhere, and are also suitable for pregnant women. It is important to choose a soft, light fabric; otherwise the pants are too bulky.

## VARIATIONS
Regular pants legs, gathered to a cuff, with a cord or elastic drawn through a casing, or a three-quarter length joined to a tight-fitting calf section so that the effect is similar to riding pants.

## FABRIC REQUIRED
2 1/2 yards (2.30 m), 36 inches (90 cm) or 45 inches (115 cm) wide.

## ENLARGING OR REDUCING PATTERN
Sizes 18 to 20: add 1/2 inches (1 1/4 cm) along all the sides; size 10 to 12: take off 1/2 inch (1 1/4 cm) all around.

## CUTTING
Lay the pattern on the folded material and cut out, allowing 5/8 inch (1 1/2 cm) extra for the seams and 2 inches (5 cm) extra at the bottom. For the casing, cut a strip of material 39 inches (97 1/2 cm) by 4 inches (10 cm), and for the belt a strip 60 inches (150 cm) by 1 1/2 inches (3 3/4 cm).
**Puffed leg with cuff** If the cuff must fit over a boot, measure the boot loosely around the ankle and then add at least 1 1/4 inches (3 cm).
**For pants with straight calf** If these will be worn with boots, measure the boot loosely around the calf. If they will be worn with low shoes, then measure your leg around the calf. In both cases, add about 5/8 inches (1 1/2 cm) extra.

## SEWING
Pin and sew the inside leg seams together. Do this once for the left leg and once for the right leg. Press the seam edges open. Pin and stitch the outside leg seams. Now pin the crotch seam together—begin at the crotch and pin the seam of the left pants leg exactly to the seam of the right pants leg. Then pin the back and front together, leaving 4 inches (10 cm) open at the center front. Press the seam edges open. Sew the casing on with the right side against the right side of the pants. Press the seam edges flat and upward, and press the casing inward, turning half its width to the inside. Then sew the casing to the inside of the pants. You will have a casing about 1 1/2 inches (3 3/4 cm) wide. Sew another line of stitching along the center line of the casing, then draw the belt, which is about 1/2 inch (1 1/4 cm) wide, through the lower casing so that a ruffle effect is created.

For the three different ways of finishing the bottom pants leg: Measure the length of the pants leg and hem, or make a cuff to which the pants leg is gathered, or draw a cord or elastic through the hem.
**Riding pants** Gather in the lower pants leg up to the dotted line. Sew the side seams of the straight calf section and press the seam edges open. Gather in the bottom of the wide pants leg and sew to the narrow calf section, adjusting the gathers evenly. Measure for the desired length of the pants leg and hem.

♥♥

Open sided Pinafore, size 12
for enlarging or reducing, see text.

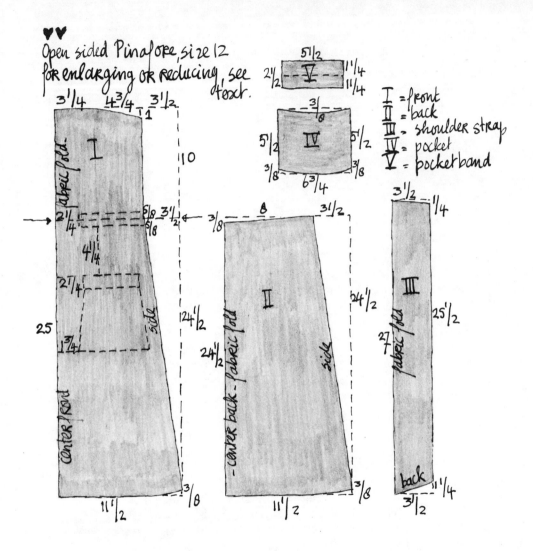

I = front
II = back
III = shoulder strap
IV = pocket
V = pocketband

The front and back sections are joined by wide, crossed shoulder straps. The pinafore hangs from the chest by the shoulder straps. The back is secured with a cord around the waist that ties at the left. The front is secured with strips that tie at the center back.

## FABRIC REQUIRED
$2\frac{1}{8}$ yards ($1\frac{9}{10}$ m), 36 inches (90 cm) wide; or $1\frac{7}{8}$ yards ($1\frac{3}{4}$ m), 45 inches (115 cm) or 54 inches (140 cm) wide.

## ENLARGING OR REDUCING PATTERN
For each change in size, add or subtract $\frac{1}{2}$ inch ($1\frac{1}{4}$ cm) along the sides of both front and back. At the top of the front, add (enlarge) or subtract (reduce) $\frac{1}{4}$ inch ($\frac{5}{8}$ cm) per size change.

## CUTTING
Lay the pattern pieces with the "fabric fold" against the folded edge of the doubled-over material. Cut out with a $\frac{5}{8}$-inch ($1\frac{1}{2}$-cm) seam allowance. Cut the shoulder strap out twice from the folded material, and likewise the pocket pieces. For the two belts, cut two strips of cloth 34 inches (85 cm) by 3 inches ($7\frac{1}{2}$ cm), including a $\frac{1}{2}$-inch ($1\frac{1}{4}$-cm) seam allowance along each side. For a pinafore with a band of contrasting material at the bottom, cut 6 inches (15 cm) from the front and back pieces at the hemline and cut an identical strip from other material. For the pinafore with a flounced strip at the hem, cut a strip of fabric 48 inches (120 cm) long by $4\frac{3}{4}$ inches (12 cm) wide. And for the trimmed skirt, cut straight edging about 3 inches ($7\frac{1}{2}$ cm) wide.

## SEWING
Along the front and back sides either stitch a narrow hem or trim with straight-cut edging. Gather the top of the front in to 12 inches (30 cm), adjusting the gathers evenly. Trim the top with straight-cut edging measuring $12\frac{1}{2}$ inches (32 cm) by 3 inches ($7\frac{1}{2}$ cm)—12 inches (30 cm) by $1\frac{1}{4}$ inches (3 cm) finished. Sew on with right sides facing, press back, and sew the trim to the wrong side with small stitches. Fold the belt double with the right sides facing, sew together leaving a small opening, turn right side out, and press flat. Pin them to the pinafore front at the right and left sides where indicated. Sew on at both upper and lower edges. This forms a sort of casing. Pull a piece of elastic about $\frac{5}{8}$ inches ($1\frac{1}{2}$ cm) wide through it and sew it fast on one side. Pull the elastic out to about $4\frac{3}{4}$ inches (12 cm) to gather in the waist a bit, and then sew it securely on the other side. Trim the top of the back piece with a piece of overlay about $1\frac{1}{2}$ inches ($3\frac{3}{4}$ cm) wide. Run a line of stitching across the back, $\frac{5}{8}$ inch ($1\frac{1}{2}$ cm) from the top edge and draw a piece of elastic $\frac{5}{8}$ inch ($1\frac{1}{2}$ cm) wide through the resultant casing. Sew it fast at one side, draw it out to about 13 inches (33 cm) and sew fast on the other side. On the left side of the back piece at the waist, sew on a strip of twill tape $7\frac{3}{4}$ inches (20 cm) long, and at the right side a strip $23\frac{1}{2}$ inches (60 cm) long to tie the back around the waist at the left. Fold the shoulder straps double lengthwise with the right sides facing. Sew together leaving a small opening, turn right side out, and press. Pin, then sew the straps to the front. Cross them at the back, and pin and sew them to the back waist, adjoining one another.

**Pockets** Sew together with the right sides facing, leaving the tops open. Snip notches into the seam edge corners, turn right side out, and press. Gather the tops in to $5\frac{1}{2}$ inches (14 cm), adjusting the gathers evenly. Lay the trim (pocket band piece) with the right side facing that of the pocket, and sew them together. Press flat, fold back, and with small stitches sew the band to the inside of the pocket. Sew the pockets to the pinafore front where indicated. Hem the bottom of the pinafore, trim, or sew on either a gathered or straight band of edging.

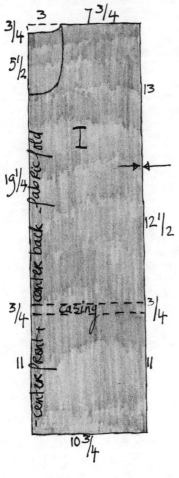

3     7³/₄

3/4

5¹/₂

13

I

19¹/₄   — Pabric fold —

— Center back —

12¹/₂

3/4    — casing —    3/4

— center front —

11           11

10³/₄

♥

Sleeveless Tunic size 16
for enlarging or Reducing, see text.
I = front + backsides
( high neckline = back
low neckline = front)

Made from one long rectangular piece of material, without shoulder seams, the only seams being those on either side. A casing with belt at the hips and casings at the shoulders through which small cords can be drawn provide shape.

## VARIATIONS
Fully sewn side seams or slit from the casing down, or the right side seam fully sewn and the left slit with loops through which a ribbon is drawn to close.

## FABRIC REQUIRED
$2\frac{1}{4}$ yards (2 m), 36 inches (90 cm) wide.

## ENLARGING OR REDUCING PATTERN
For each change in size add or subtract $\frac{1}{2}$ inch ($1\frac{1}{4}$ cm) at the side; enlarge or reduce the neckline by $\frac{1}{4}$ inch ($\frac{5}{8}$ cm) per size change; reduce or enlarge the hip casing by $\frac{1}{4}$ inch ($\frac{5}{8}$ cm) per size change.

## CUTTING
Fold the material double twice, first folding lengthwise and then along the width. Lay the pattern with the "fabric folds" against the folded edges of the material. Cut out with a $\frac{5}{8}$-inch ($1\frac{1}{2}$-cm) seam allowance. Make a small notch at the arrow in the side as an indication of how far the seam is to be sewn. Also make two small notches where the casing starts. First cut out the high back neckline, then unfold the material along its length and cut out the low neckline on one side. For the shoulder casings, cut two strips $8\frac{1}{4}$ inches (21 cm) by $1\frac{1}{2}$ inches ($3\frac{3}{4}$ cm); for the casing at the hips, a strip 43 inches (108 cm) by 2 inches (5 cm); and for the belt, a strip 60 inches (150 cm) by $1\frac{1}{2}$ inches ($3\frac{3}{4}$ cm).

## SEWING
Pin front and back together at the sides and sew from the notch down to the casing. Press the seam edges flat. Press a sharp crease exactly along the shoulder line. Now, in front of the crease, pin on the right and left shoulder casings—to be about $\frac{5}{8}$ inch ($1\frac{1}{2}$ cm) wide finished. Leave the ends open. At the outside edge of the shoulder, where the casing ends, stitch on a ribbon about 10 inches (25 cm) long by $\frac{1}{2}$ inch ($1\frac{1}{4}$ cm) wide. Now, from the neck, draw a ribbon measuring about $17\frac{1}{2}$ inches (45 cm) by $\frac{1}{2}$ inch ($1\frac{1}{4}$ cm) through each of the casings. Stitch across the neck end of the casings to secure this ribbon. Tie it to the other ribbon, of 10 inches (25 cm) length, at the outside shoulder, gathering it in a little. Trim the neckline with edging cut on the bias. Pin and sew on the casing at the hips where indicated. Leave an opening of about 2 inches (5 cm) at the center front. Make a belt about $\frac{1}{2}$ inch ($1\frac{1}{4}$ cm) wide and draw it through the casing. Finish off the slits and the bottom with a rolled hem. Finish the armholes with a rolled hem.

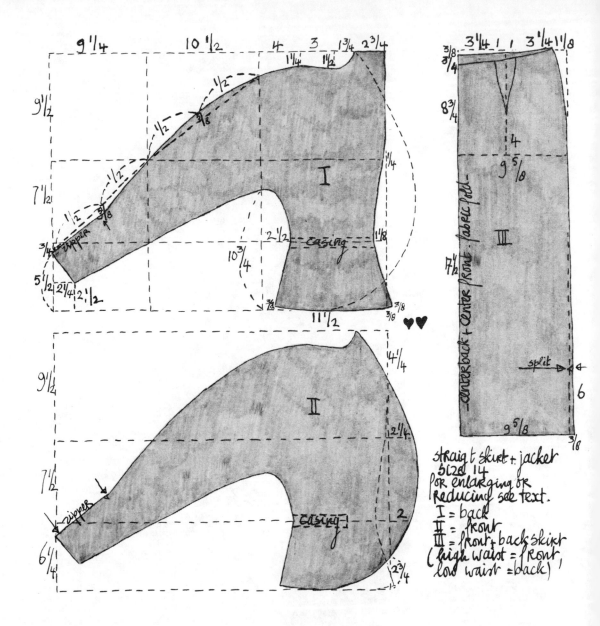

9 1/4    10 1/2    4    3    1 3/4  2 3/4
1 1/4    1 1/2
1/2
9 1/2
1/2    1/2    1/8    1/4
7 1/2
1/2    1/8    1/2
3/4    zipper    I    casing    1 1/8
5 1/2  2 1/4  2 1/2    10 3/4    2 1/2    casing
3/8    11 1/2    3/8  3/8    ❤❤

4 1/4
9 1/2
II    2 1/4
7 1/2    zipper    casing    2
6 1/4    2 3/4

3/8  3 1/4  1  1  3 1/4  1 1/8
3/8
3/4
8 3/4
4
9 5/8
III
7 1/2    centerback + center front, fabric fold
split
6
9 5/8    3/8

straight skirt + jacket
size 14
for enlarging or
reducing see text.
I = back
II = front
III = front + back skirt
(high waist = front,
low waist = back)

# STRAIGHT SKIRT AND JACKET

A straight skirt with slit sides, and a short jacket with short sleeves or with long sleeves that fit snugly at the wrists with a zipper closing. The sleeves are "too long" and therefore will come out somewhat puffed.

## VARIATIONS

On the inside of the jacket at the waist is a stitched-in casing with an elastic. On the outside at the waist is a belt drawn through loops at the side seams. The casing can also be sewn to the outside of the jacket and then a belt drawn through. The jacket can be made in brocade, satin, lace, or some other dressy fabric for use in the evening, or in tweed, linen, cotton, etc., for day wear.

## FABRIC REQUIRED

**Jacket** 2¾ yards (2½ m), 36 inches (90 cm) wide.
**Skirt** 1¾ yards (1⁶⁄₁₀ m), 36 inches (90 cm) wide.

## ENLARGING OR REDUCING PATTERN

**Jacket** Add or subtract ½ inch (1¼ cm) at the side seams for each change in size. Add or subtract ¼ inch (⁵⁄₈ cm) along the undersleeve seam and at the shoulder seam for each size change.
**Skirt** Add or subtract ½ inch (1¼ cm) per size change at the center front and back lines. The dart in the back must always lie in the center of each back piece.

## CUTTING

Draw the skirt pattern once with the lower waistline and dart—this is the back—and once with the high waist and no dart—the front. Lay all pattern pieces on the folded fabric and cut out with a ⁵⁄₈-inch (1½-cm) seam allowance and 3 inches (7½ cm) extra for the skirt hem.

## SEWING

**Skirt** Stitch the darts in the skirt. Pin the side seams together and sew together, except for the top 7 inches (18 cm) on the left side for the zipper, and only as far down as the arrow for the slits. Press the seam edges open and sew in the zipper. Measure the desired waist length, cut a waistband about 2½ inches (6¼ cm) wide, and allow 2 inches (5 cm) extra for a turnover. Sew on the waistband, reinforced first with iron-on tape, to the skirt. Fold the top half over to the wrong side and sew fast there. Finish off the slits and skirt bottom.

**Jacket** Stitch the center seam. Pin the front to the back and sew together along the shoulder, underarm, and side seams. Use a very fine zigzag stitch, because the top sleeve edges are cut on the bias and therefore prone to stretching. Leave open the bottom 6 inches (15 cm) on the sleeves for the zipper. Be sure to clip the seam edge curves at the neck, armpits, and the waist. Press the seam edges open. If making a casing at the waist, cut a strip of material 27½ inches (70 cm) by 1½ inches (3¾ cm) and sew on where indicated. Draw a piece of elastic or a narrow belt through it. Trim the jacket center front and bottom with a bias-cut strip of the same or contrasting material (e.g., satin). Make closures with snap fasteners, a brooch, or buttons and buttonholes, and a sewn-on or separate belt that goes through loops at the sides and center back. Finish the sleeve bottoms and put in the zippers.

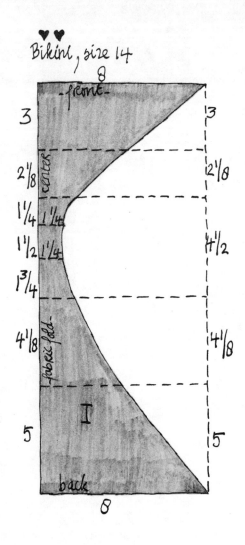

♥ ♥
Bikini, size 14

8

front

3                     3

2 1/8   center            2 1/8

1 1/4   1 1/4

1 1/2   1 1/4          4 1/2

1 3/4

4 1/8   fabric fold       4 1/8

5    I                  5

back

8

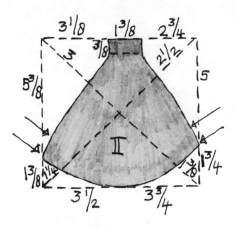

3 1/8    1 3/8    2 3/4

3    3/8         2 1/2

5 3/8                5

II

1 3/8 1 1/4           7/8 1 3/4

3 1/2        3 5/4

For enlarging or reducing, see text.
I = panty (cut 2x)
II = bra (cut 4x)

# BIKINI

The advantage of a bikini you make yourself is that you can, if desired, make the panty and the bra in different sizes. The bikini is lined, either with the same fabric or perhaps with a light white cotton. The bra is supported by cording tied at the center back and at the back of the neck. The panty is cut from one piece and tied with cords at the sides. Suitable fabric would be a soft cotton, a stretch terry, cotton tricot, silk jersey, etc. A bikini made in a stretch fabric is more comfortable.

## FABRIC REQUIRED
1$\frac{3}{8}$ yards (1$\frac{1}{4}$ m), 36 inches (90 cm) wide.

## ENLARGING OR REDUCING PATTERN
The pattern drawn here is size 14.

**In general** For the panty add or subtract $\frac{3}{8}$ inch ($\frac{3}{4}$ cm) per size change at the front and back top sides. At the sides, draw a line that tapers gradually from the crotch to $\frac{3}{8}$ inch ($\frac{3}{4}$ cm), more or less at the top per change in size—outward for enlarging, inward for reducing [see pattern].

**Bra** Along the bottom edges add or subtract $\frac{3}{8}$ inch ($\frac{3}{4}$ cm) per size change. At the sides, taper a line out or in to $\frac{3}{8}$ inch ($\frac{3}{4}$ cm), more or less at the bottom edge per size change [see pattern].

## CUTTING
Lay the pattern pieces with the "fabric fold" against the folded edge of the doubled-over material. Cut the panty out twice, allowing $\frac{1}{2}$ inch (1$\frac{1}{4}$ cm) extra for seams except at the upper front edge; no seam allowance at the front. Cut the bra out twice from the folded material, with a $\frac{1}{2}$-inch (1$\frac{1}{4}$-cm) seam allowance.

## SEWING
**Panty** Sew together around outer edges, leaving open at top front and where indicated between arrows, $\frac{5}{8}$ inch (1$\frac{1}{2}$ cm) at each side of top back edge [see pattern]. Trim seam edges to $\frac{1}{4}$ inch ($\frac{5}{8}$ cm), turn right side out, press flat, and run a row of stitching about $\frac{1}{8}$ inch (1 mm) in from all sewn edges (i.e., do not stitch the top front or open areas at top back). Run a second row of stitching parallel to the first, and about $\frac{3}{8}$ inch ($\frac{3}{4}$ cm) in from it to form casings. Run a $\frac{1}{4}$-inch ($\frac{5}{8}$-cm) piece of elastic through each leg and stitch fast at front edges, leaving loose at the back temporarily. Draw a third piece of elastic through the top back casing, and pull out all three pieces at the back side edges, so that each leg measures about 4 inches (10 cm) smaller than originally, and the back edge about 2 inches (5 cm) smaller. Stitch the ends of the elastic securely to each back opening and trim off close to stitching. Over this, sew a piece of cording about 10 inches (25 cm) long to each side. Bind the top front edge with a matching piece of bias cording about 35 inches (88 cm) long, so that a 10-inch (25-cm) long "ribbon" extends at either side, to be tied with the cording at the back.

**Bra** Pin the bra and bra lining together with right sides facing. Sew together all around except for the small straight tab edge and the $\frac{5}{8}$ inch (1$\frac{1}{2}$ cm) at the right and left bottom between the arrows [see pattern]. Trim the seam edges back to $\frac{1}{4}$ inch ($\frac{5}{8}$ cm). Sew a line of stitching around $\frac{1}{8}$ inch (1 mm) from the edge, leaving the space between the arrows open at the bottom right and left. Now sew a second line of stitching at the bottom, about $\frac{3}{8}$ inch ($\frac{3}{4}$ cm) from the first line, to form a sort of casing. **Note** Be careful not to make two left or two right cups. Through the casing at the cup bottom, draw a piece of cording 48 inches (120 cm) long by $\frac{3}{8}$ inch ($\frac{3}{4}$ cm) wide. Gather in the tabs at the top of the cups to about $\frac{1}{2}$ inch (1$\frac{1}{4}$ cm) and sew to shoulder straps made from cording 20 inches (50 cm) long, which then tie together in back of the neck.

♥

Beach Cover-ups Size 10
for enlarging or Reducing, see text.

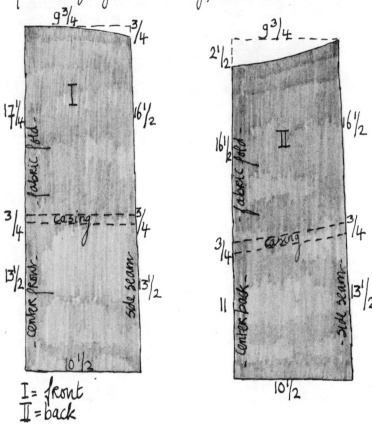

9¾ --- ¾

I

17¼          16½

¾  --- casing --- ¾

13½                13½
        side seam
center front

10½

9¾

2½

II

16½          16½

¾  casing  ¾

11    center back    side seam    13½

10½

I = front
II = back

# BEACH COVER-UPS

An easy-to-make dress or blouse, gathered in above the breasts by means of a cord drawn through a sewn-on casing plus frill. The cord is tied at the center front, and the ends may or may not be tied at the back of the neck.

## VARIATIONS
A dress with a casing and belt at the hips; a balloon dress with elastic or a cord drawn through the hem; or two dresses over each other, one worn as a skirt and the other as a blouse, with or without slits.

## FABRIC REQUIRED
2 yards (1¾ m), 36 inches (90 cm) wide.

## ENLARGING OR REDUCING PATTERN
Add or subtract ½ inch (1¼ cm) at the side seams per size change.

## CUTTING
Lay the pattern pieces with the "fabric fold" against the folded edge of the doubled-over material. Cut with a ⅝-inch (1½-cm) allowance for side seams, ½ inch (1¼ cm) extra along the top, and 2½ inches (6¼ cm) extra for the hem. For the frilled casing at the top, cut a strip 44 inches (110 cm) by 3 inches (7½ cm) for size 10. Add or subtract 1½ inches (3¾ cm) in length per size change. For any other casing, cut a strip of material 44 inches (110 cm) by 1½ inches (3¾ cm), and for a belt a strip 60 inches (150 cm) by 1½ inches (3¾ cm).

## SEWING
Stitch side seams together. Press the seam edges open. Pin the casing strip for the top to the dress top with right sides facing. Turn under the casing ends to the inside for about the last ½ inch (1¼ cm), making the ends meet at the center front, to form an opening through which a cord can be drawn. Sew the strip along the top edge. Press the seam edges flat upward, then fold the strip to the inside for half its width. Press and sew fast. You now have a casing about 1¼ inches (3 cm) wide. In the precise center of it, sew a line of stitching all around to create two casings, each ⅝ inch (1½ cm) wide. Through the bottom casing, draw a piece of elastic 11½ inches (30 cm) long and ½ inch (1¼ cm) wide, with a piece of ribbon or lacing 20 inches (50 cm) long sewn to each end. For the optional casing at the hips, sew on a strip of material, leaving the center front open for 2 inches (5 cm). Make a belt from ½ inch (1¼ cm) to ¾ inch (1⅞ cm) wide to draw through this casing. Measure the desired length to the bottom and hem.

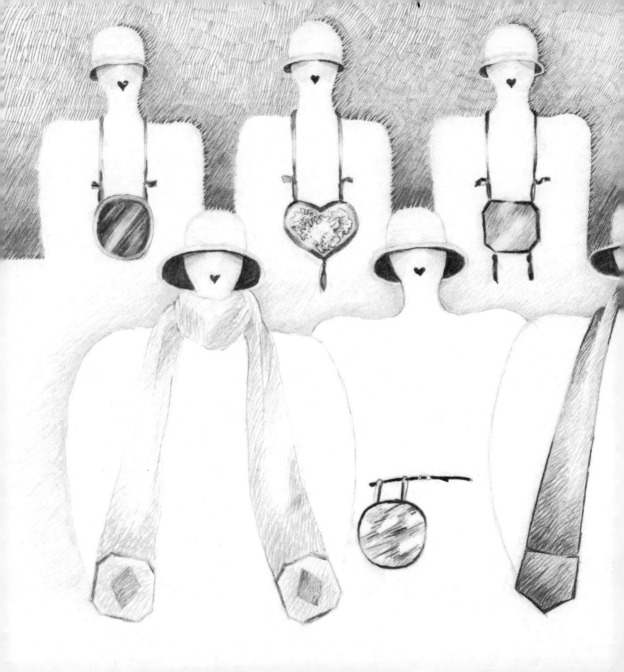

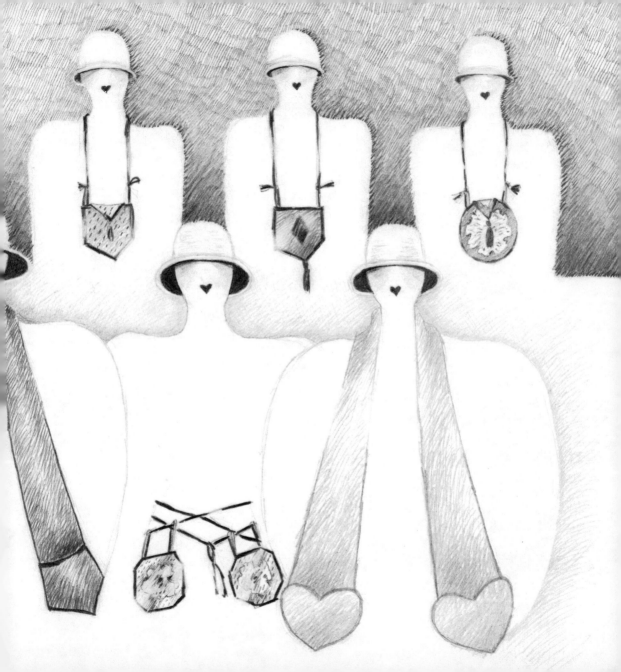

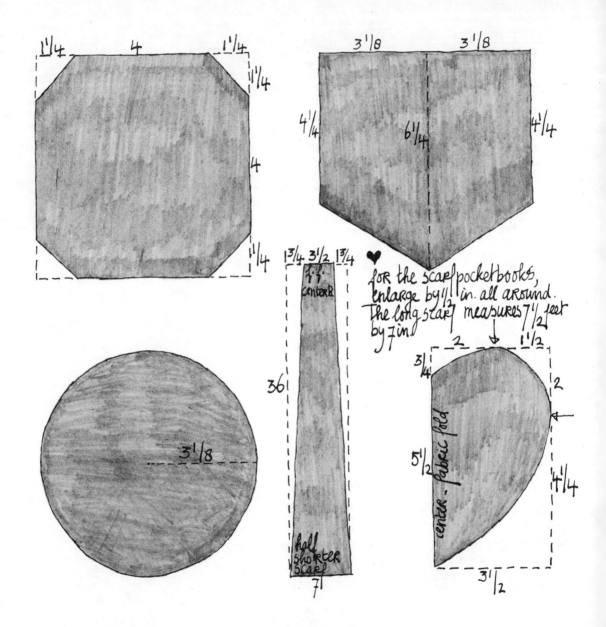

1¼  4  1¼
1¼
4
1¼

3¹⁄8  3¹⁄8
4¼  6¹⁄4  4¼

1¾ 3½ 1¾
center B

36

3¹⁄8

full shorter scarf
7

♥ for the scarf pocketbooks, enlarge by 1½ in. all around. The long scarf measures 7½ feet by 7 in.

2  1½
¾
2
center - fabric fold
5½
4¼
3½

# POCKETBOOKS

A heart, an octagon, a circle, and a pointed shape. Four little pocketbooks with loops attached that can be worn in different ways:

1. With a cord or ribbon tied to the loops, worn around the neck
2. Hanging by the loops from a belt
3. One or two worn on a sewn band wrapped around the waist two or three times and then tied (worn like pockets)
4. As scarf pocketbooks, enlarged all around by $\frac{1}{2}$ inch (1$\frac{1}{4}$ cm), and sewn to a long scarf or sewn to a somewhat shorter piece of neckwear—narrow at the neck and flaring out at the bottom. The long scarf is wrapped around the neck once and then hangs down on the left and right sides.

## FABRIC REQUIRED

For the pocketbooks: 18 inches (46 cm), 36 inches (90 cm) wide, plus an equal amount for both lining and interfacing. For the scarf: 2 yards (1$\frac{3}{4}$ m), 36 inches (90 cm) wide if it is to be cut in one single piece.

## ENLARGING PATTERN

For the scarf pocketbooks, enlarge by $\frac{1}{2}$ inch (1$\frac{1}{4}$ cm) all around.

## CUTTING

Cut the pocketbook out twice without seam allowance, and also twice from a lining fabric and an iron-on material.

## SEWING

Press the iron-on pieces to the wrong sides of the cutout pocketbooks. Decorate if desired with an appliqué or perhaps some embroidery. Baste on the lining. Sew fast all around with a zigzag stitch, once for the front and once for the back piece of the pocketbook. Press. Trim front and back all around with a bias-cut edging, and press. Now sew front and back sides together, leaving the top side open between the arrows. Sew on a button and button loop for closing, or press the flap forward and then add a button and button loop. Then sew on the supporting loops, one end to the front and one to the back—one loop on the left, one on the right. Then make either a ribbon-type support for around the neck or around the waist.

**Scarf Pocketbooks** Cut the ends of the scarf into the shape of the bottom of the desired pocketbook.

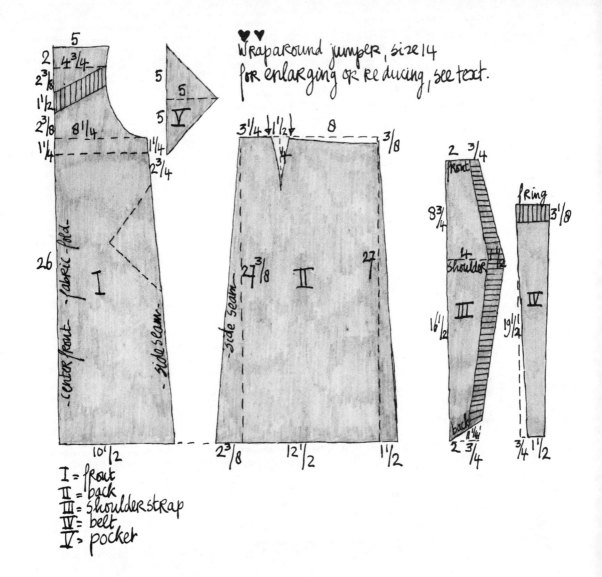

Wraparound jumper, size 14
for enlarging or reducing, see text.

I = front
II = back
III = shoulderstrap
IV = belt
V = pocket

# WRAPAROUND JUMPER

A wraparound jumper with wide flaring shoulder straps that cross at the back.

## VARIATIONS

Pockets, belt, shoulder straps, and the V-shaped front piece can be trimmed with a contrasting color or made from a contrasting fabric or suede. Fringes are another possibility.

## FABRIC REQUIRED

2¼ yards (2 m), 36 inches (90 cm) or 45 inches (115 cm) wide.

## ENLARGING OR REDUCING PATTERN

Add ½ inch (1¼ cm) at the side seams per size change to enlarge, or subtract to reduce. Add or subtract ¼ inch (⅝ cm) per size change along the top and sides of the front piece, and ¼ inch (⅝ cm) along the top sides of the back.

## CUTTING

Lay the pattern pieces with the "fabric fold" against the folded edge of the doubled-over material. Cut the front piece once and the other pieces twice from the folded fabric. As an overlay for the top front, cut out the top front pattern down to the dotted line. Cut out the top 1¼ inches (3 cm) of the back pattern as an overlay for the back. Allow ⅝ inch (1½ cm) extra for seams and 2½ inches (6¼ cm) for the hem. For a jumper that is to be trimmed, cut pockets, shoulder straps, belt, and the front panel without a seam allowance; although, do allow 2 inches (5 cm) extra length for shoulder strap seams at the ends.

## SEWING

**The trimmed jumper** Lay shoulder straps, front panel, and pocket pieces against each other, wrong sides facing, and trim with bias-cut trim—bias tape, bias-cut satin binding, etc. Pin the front panel to the top front and sew fast along the trim. Stitch the side seams of the front and back together and to the side seams of the overlay. Press the seam edges open.

Finish the outer edges of the back pieces with a rolled hem, then pin the overlay on with the right side facing the right side of the main piece. Stitch together, making certain that your line of stitching begins and ends where the already trimmed front panel is sewn fast. Cut the seam allowance back to ½ inch (1¼ cm), and snip notches into the curves. Turn right side out, flatten, and press. Then run a line of stitching ½ inch (1¼ cm) in from the edge. Make buttonholes at the left and right of the front panel top. Fold the shoulder straps double, wrong sides facing. Finish the diagonally cut sides with trim, then do the same with the belt pieces. Sew the ends of the belt pieces fast to the top of the back. At the side seam of the left back side, make a buttonhole large enough to draw the belt through. Try the jumper on—pull one belt through the buttonhole and tie it securely at the center front. Attach a pin to the middle of the left back. Take off the jumper and pin the shoulder straps to the right and left of this pin so that they cross in the back. Check that the length of the shoulder straps is right, then sew them fast. Sew buttons to the shoulder straps. Baste the pocket pieces together, wrong sides facing, finish the outer edges with trim, press, and sew on where indicated.

**Jumper with pockets, shoulder straps, and front panel in a contrasting color** The instructions are virtually the same as above, except that pockets, shoulder straps, and front panel are made as follows: Lay the pattern pieces together with right sides facing and sew together, leaving an opening for turning right side out. Snip into the angles of the seam edges, cut the seam allowance back to ¼ inch (⅝ cm), turn right side out, flatten, press, and run a line of stitching ¼ inch (⅝ cm) in from the edge around each piece.

**Fringe** This can be cut from a soft leather or suede [see pattern].

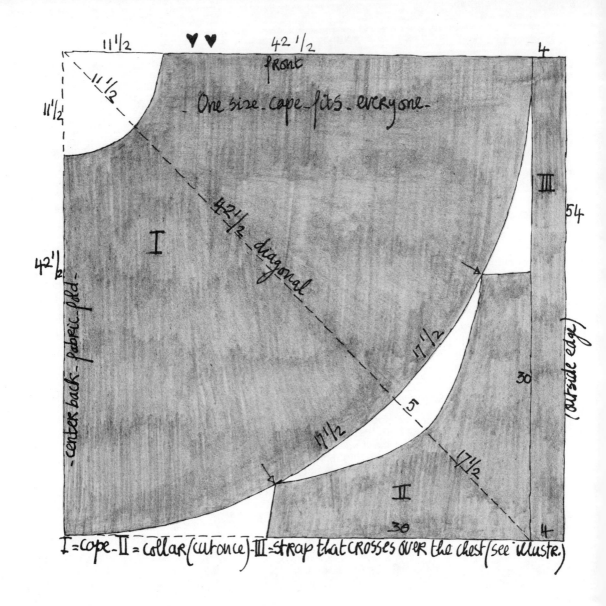

One size · cape · fits · everyone ·

11½

11½

11½

11½

42½ front

4

III

54

42½ — diagonal

(outside edge)

I

17½

5

30

17½

17½

42½

— center back — fabric fold —

II

30

4

30

I = cape · II = collar (cut once) · III = strap that crosses over the chest (see illustr.)

# CAPE

A cape cut from a half circle. The collar is cut from the remnant piece. They are both gathered in at the neckline and sewn to a curved strip of material. The straps that cross over the chest are sewn to this strip. They cross again in the back and then are tied fast at the front center waist; the inspiration is the English nurse's cape. The choice of fabric determines the character of the cape—trimmed with satin (an evening cape), made of wool, or perhaps of nylon (for a rain cape).

## FABRIC REQUIRED

$3\frac{1}{3}$ yards (3 m), 54 inches (135 cm) wide.

## CUTTING

Fold the material in half widthwise and lay it down flat—on the floor, if you will. Be sure the two halves align exactly. Then with a sharp tailor's chalk draw on the pattern. First measure a square 54 inches (135 cm) by 54 inches (135 cm) on the material starting from the fold. You will be left with two 4-inch (10-cm) strips along the outside for the straps. Cut this off so that you are left with the square [see pattern]. As a guide, draw a straight line diagonally between two opposite corners [see pattern]. Then draw an arc with a radius of $11\frac{1}{2}$ inches (29 cm). For a compass, use a tape measure or a string with a piece of chalk attached. Then draw an arc with a radius of 54 inches (135 cm), measuring from the same point. Now draw the collar [see pattern]. Cut out the cape exactly as drawn, thus with no seam allowance. Then cut the collar out once from a single layer of fabric. From the remaining fabric cut a curved strip 22 inches (55 cm) long and $2\frac{1}{2}$ inches ($6\frac{1}{4}$ cm) wide, cutting along the curve that resulted from cutting out the bottom of the cape.

## SEWING

Gather the top of the cape and the collar in to 20 inches (50 cm). Pin and baste them together. Sew the curved strip on here, turn in to the inside, and sew to the inside of the cape by hand. Finish the center front and bottom of the cape with a rolled hem or with bias-cut trim—leather, satin, wool, etc. Sew the straps, $1\frac{1}{2}$ inches ($3\frac{3}{4}$ cm) wide when finished, to the curved strip at the top left front openings.

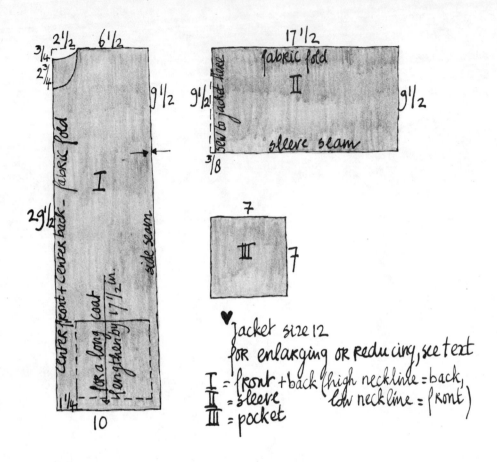

2¹/₂    6¹/₂

³/₄
2³/₄

9¹/₂

I

center front + center back - fabric fold

29¹/₂

side seam

for a long coat lengthen by 17¹/₂ in.

1¹/₄

10

17¹/₂
fabric fold

II

9¹/₂    sew to jacket here    9¹/₂

sleeve seam

³/₈

7

III    7

♥ jacket size 12
for enlarging or reducing, see text
I = front + back (high neckline = back,
II = sleeve          low neckline = front)
III = pocket

A long jacket that you can easily lengthen into a coat. It is a "between seasons" jacket or one to be worn over heavy sweaters. A fringed travel blanket or a regular blanket is very suitable, but naturally the jacket can be made of other materials as well. The center front is closed with lacing or braided ribbon.

## VARIATIONS

Long or short, trimmed with satin or self-made edging of a contrasting material or leather or suede, or finished with wool yarn in a blanket or feather stitch.

## FABRIC REQUIRED

**Jacket** 1⅔ yards (1½ m), 45 inches (115 cm) or 54 inches (135 cm) wide; or a travel blanket 60 inches (1½ m) by 48 inches (120 cm).
**Coat** 2¼ yards (2 m), 45 inches (115 cm) or 54 inches (135 cm) wide; or a travel blanket 80 inches (2 m) by 48 inches (120 cm).

## ENLARGING OR REDUCING PATTERN

Add (enlarge) or subtract (reduce) ¹/₂ inch (1¼ cm) at the side seams per change in size. Enlarge or reduce the neckline by ¼ inch (⅝ cm) per size change. For the sleeves, add or subtract ½ inch (1¼ cm) at the seam per size change.

## CUTTING

Lay the pattern pieces with the "fabric fold" against the folded edge of the doubled-over material. Center front need not be cut on the fold, but if it is, slit the fold open afterward. If the jacket is to be made from a travel blanket, lay the bottom of the coat (front and back) and the sleeve end against the fringe. Cut with a ⅝-inch (1½-cm) seam allowance. Cut nothing extra at the neckline, center front, or for the pockets.

## SEWING

First sew a zigzag stitch around all edges. Sew front and back together at the shoulder seam. Press the seam edges open. Now, on both sides of the shoulder seam, sew a line of stitching parallel to it ¼ inch (⅝ cm) from the seam. Pin and sew the sleeves to the front and back at arrows. Then pin and sew together the side seams of the jacket and the sleeve, reinforcing at the armpit with an extra line of stitching, snipping the seam edges in to the seam line. Finish the center front, neckline, and pockets with a decorative stitch or trim with bias-cut trim. Sew on the pockets. Sew the closure laces onto the center front—braid cords or make ties either from the same material as the jacket or the trim.

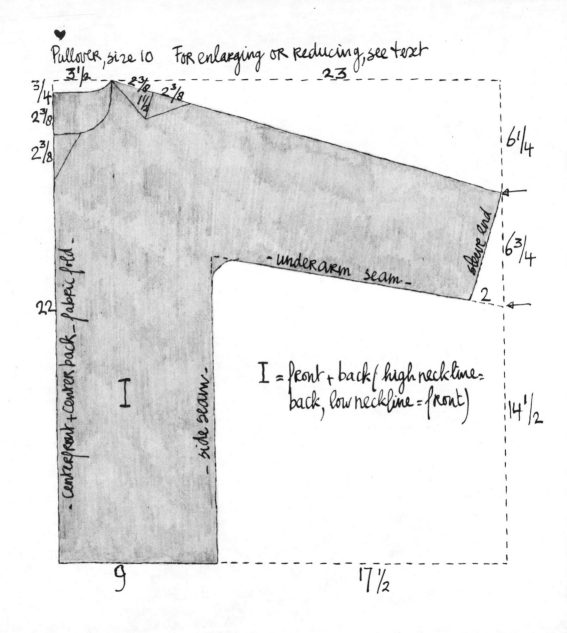

Pullover, size 10   For enlarging or reducing, see text

3½   23

¾   2¾   2⅜
2⅜   1½
2⅜

6¼

sleeve end

6¾

2

— underarm seam —

— centre front + centre back — fabric fold —

22

— side seam —

I

I = front + back ( high neckline =
back, low neckline = front )

14½

9   17½

# PULLOVERS

A pullover of wool or cotton jersey, or of any stretchable knit weave. Possibly decorated with suede sew-on patches and/or hand-knit cuffs.

## VARIATIONS

Hand-knit cuffs of the same or contrasting color as the sweater. Knit cuffs with a knit-2, purl-2 stitch and about 6¾ inches (17 cm) long. Or knit a gigantic turtleneck collar, or a small collar about 1 inch (2½ cm) wide, and finish the neckline with that. Draw a small cord through the sleeve ends, or sew on a double-thickness fabric edging that can be turned back. Decorate the neckline with suede patches or sew patches along the sleeve seam. Make with or without side slits. Or make it a blouson pullover by drawing an elastic through the bottom hem, or gather the sweater onto a wide waistband that may be open at the left and then be laced closed (optional).

## FABRIC REQUIRED

1¾ yards (1⁶⁄₁₀ m), 54 inches (135 cm) or 60 inches (1½ m) wide.

## ENLARGING OR REDUCING PATTERN

Add (enlarge) or subtract (reduce) ½ inch (1¼ cm) per size change along the bottom, side seam underarm seam, and sleeve end. Enlarge or reduce the neckline by ¼ inch (⅝ cm) per size change.

## SEWING

Lay the front and back pieces together with right sides facing. Pin and sew together with a tight zig-zag stitch (to give along with the stretch in the fabric, use synthetic thread). Cut seam edges back to ¼ inch (⅝ cm), then sew together with a wide zig-zag stitch. Press flat carefully. Zigzag around the neckline (without stretching the fabric). Sew on the turtleneck or small collar. Or sew by hand a rolled hem that comes somewhat to the outside. Sew on any suede patches.

**Finishing the sleeve end** To sew on the hand-knit cuffs, gather in the sleeve end to about the width of the forearm, dividing the pleats evenly. Pin the cuff to it, stretching the cuff slightly if necessary. Sew on with a zigzag stitch. Pull out the basting thread and stitch over a second time with a zigzag stitch. Or sew on a small casing through which elastic or cording may be drawn. Or sew on a wide band of material, turn under, and sew fast to the sleeve inside by hand.

**Finishing the bottom** Hem, drawing a cord or elastic through, if desired, or gather to the hip band. Gather the bottom, adjusting gathers evenly, sew on the hip band, turn back to the wrong side, and sew fast by hand. Leave the left side closed, or open to be laced shut with a cord.

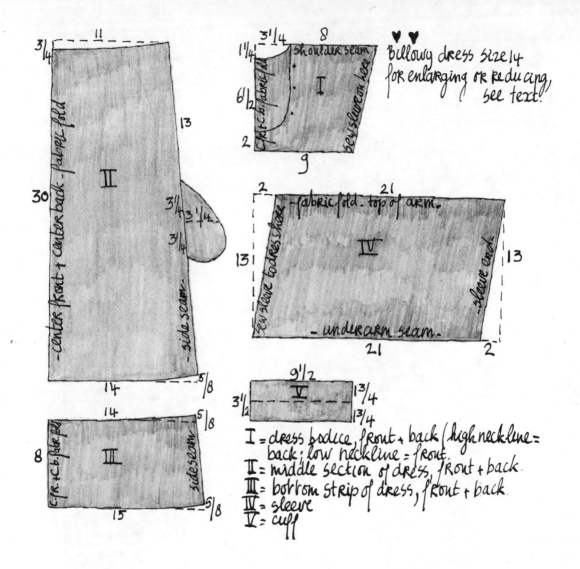

♥ ♥ Billowy dress size 14
for enlarging or reducing,
see text!

I = dress bodice, front + back (high neckline = back; low neckline = front.
II = middle section of dress, front + back.
III = bottom strip of dress, front + back.
IV = sleeve
V = cuff

# BILLOWY DRESS

The dress and sleeves are gathered onto a yoke. Almost any kind of fabric can be used for this dress, including corduroy, in combination with a quilted cotton, or various flower designs. Made long, this is an ideal house or morning dress. Made of satin and worn in combination with puffed satin trousers, it becomes evening attire.

## FABRIC REQUIRED
$4^1/_2$ yards (4 m), 36 inches (90 cm) wide.

## ENLARGING OR REDUCING PATTERN
Add (enlarge) or subtract (reduce) $1/_2$ inch ($1^1/_4$ cm) per size change at the side seams. Do the same along the sides of the yoke and at the underarm seam. Add or subtract $1/_4$ inch ($5/_8$ cm) at the sleeve end per size change, and $1/_4$ inch ($5/_8$ cm) at the neckline.

## CUTTING
Lay the pattern pieces with the "fabric fold" along the folded edge of the doubled-over material, and cut out with a $5/_8$-inch ($1^1/_2$-cm) seam allowance and $2^1/_2$ inches ($6^1/_4$ cm) extra for the hem, which equals the bottom of pattern piece III.

## SEWING
Sew the shoulder seams of the yoke together and press seam edges open. Gather in the top of the front and back body sections to 18 inches (45 cm) each for size 14, adjusting the gathers evenly. Pin the front and back to the yoke front and back respectively, with the right sides facing. Sew fast and press the seam edges upward. Gather the top of the sleeves in to $19^1/_2$ inches (49 cm), adjusting the gathers evenly, then pin and sew to the yoke with the right sides facing. Pin and sew together the underarm seams, the side seams, and the pockets, and press the seam edges open. Sew the side seams of the bottom section together, then sew to the body of the dress. Measure for the desired length and hem. Finish the neckline with a bias-cut trim or with an overlay. At the center front, base of the neckline, and at the points indicated on the pattern by little dots, sew on little loops through which a lacing, measuring about 54 inches (135 cm) long by $3/_8$ inches ($3/_4$ cm) wide, can be drawn—to serve as a decorative closure that may be tied around in back of the neck. Gather the sleeve ends in to $9^1/_2$ inches (24 cm), adjusting the gathers evenly. Sew the cuff side seams together, then press the seam edges open. Baste the cuffs to the sleeve ends with the right sides facing. Sew on, press the seam edges inward, then turn half the cuff to the inside and sew by hand with fine stitches.

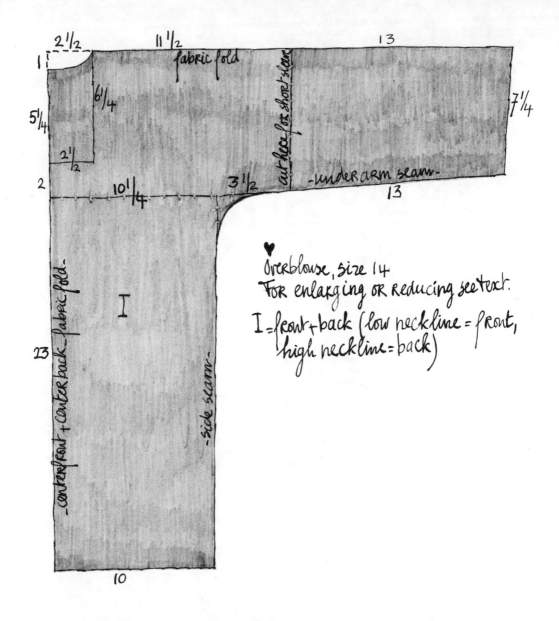

2½

1

11½

fabric fold

13

6¼

5¼

2½

2

10¼

3½

cut here for short sleeve

underarm seam

13

7¼

center front + center back – fabric fold

I

side seam

23

10

♥
Overblouse, size 14
For enlarging or reducing see text.
I = front + back (low neckline = front,
high neckline = back)

# OVERBLOUSE

An overblouse that can be made of any soft woven or knit fabric. Short or long sleeves, with or without a belt, possibly fringed at the bottom, and maybe with tricot or hand-knit bands for cuffs.

## FABRIC REQUIRED
$1\frac{7}{8}$ yards ($1\frac{3}{4}$ m), 60 inches (150 cm) wide.

## ENLARGING OR REDUCING PATTERN
Add (enlarge) or subtract (reduce) $\frac{1}{2}$ inch ($1\frac{1}{4}$ cm) per size change along the bottom, side seams, and underarm seams. Add or subtract $\frac{1}{4}$ inch ($\frac{5}{8}$ cm) at the sleeve end per size change, and $\frac{1}{4}$ inch ($\frac{5}{8}$ cm) along the neckline.

## CUTTING
Fold the material twice, once along its width and once along its length so that no shoulder seam is necessary. Cut out with a $\frac{5}{8}$-inch ($1\frac{1}{2}$-cm) seam allowance and $2\frac{1}{2}$ inches ($6\frac{1}{4}$ cm) extra at the bottom for the hem.

## SEWING
Pin and sew side seams and underarm seams. If the overblouse is made of a knit fabric, use a zigzag stitch. Press seam edges open. Finish the neckline with bias-cut trim or a rolled hem sewn by hand. Measure the body and sleeve lengths and hem. If intending a fringe (bought or homemade) and/or cuffs, sew them on. Gather the sleeve ends and sew the cuffs on with a zigzag stitch.

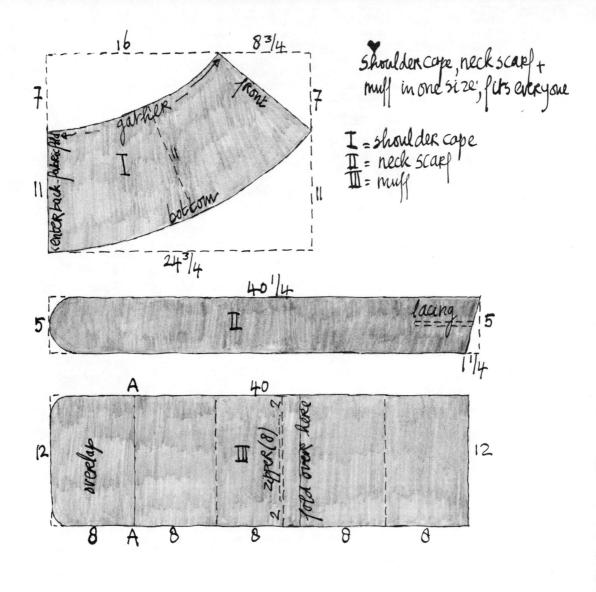

16    8¾

7    7

gather

front

center back-place fold

I

bottom

11    11

24¾

shoulder cape, neck scarf +
muff in one size; fits everyone

I = shoulder cape
II = neck scarf
III = muff

40¼

5    II    lacing    5

1¼

A    40

12    overlap    III    zipper (8)    fold over here    12

8    A    8    8    8    8

# SHOULDER CAPE, NECK SCARF, AND MUFF

One size fits everyone. They can be made of a soft, brightly colored wool fabric, with or without a contrasting lining. The shoulder cape is fastened with a collar made of lighter material (e.g., flannel) and closes at the center front with a button.

## FABRIC REQUIRED
**Shoulder cape** ⅝ yard (56 cm), 54 inches (135 cm) wide, and the same for a lining fabric. In addition, a piece of fabric ⅝ yard (56 cm) by 4 inches (10 cm) for the collar.
**Neck scarf** ¼ yard (23 cm), 45 inches (115 cm) or 54 inches (135 cm) wide, and the same for a lining fabric.
**Muff** ½ yard (45 cm), 45 inches (115 cm) or 54 inches (135 cm) wide. For the lining, a piece of fabric 10 inches (25 cm) by 14 inches (35 cm).

## CUTTING
**Shoulder cape** Lay the pattern with the "fabric fold" against the folded edge of the doubled-over material, and cut out with a ½-inch (1¼-cm) seam allowance. For the collar, cut a strip measuring 20 inches (50 cm) by 4 inches (10 cm).
**Neck scarf and muff** Lay the pattern pieces on a single thickness of material and cut out with a ½-inch (1¼-cm) seam allowance all around.

## SEWING
**Shoulder cape** Pin the lining to the cape with the right sides facing. Sew together the bottom and sides leaving top open, snip into the seam edges at the corners, and snip notches into the seam edge curve. Turn right side out, flatten, and press. Gather the neckline in to 17 inches (43 cm), adjusting the gathers evenly. Pin on the collar, right sides facing. On the right side of the collar you will need an overlap of about 1¼ inches (3 cm). Sew, press seam edges upward, fold the collar in half to the inside, and sew fast to the wrong side by hand. Make a buttonhole in the overlap and sew a button on the other collar end.

**Neck scarf** Pin the lining to the neck scarf with right sides facing. Sew together all around, leaving an opening for turning right side out. Snip into the seam edge corners, turn right side out, flatten, and press. Sew a strip of lining fabric 5½ inches (14 cm) long by ⅜ inch (¾ cm) to the diagonal end of the scarf [see pattern].
**Muff** Press a patch of iron-on backing 12 inches (30 cm) by 4 inches (10 cm) to the wrong side of the material, where the zipper is to be running the width of the muff, and centered over the zipper area [see pattern]. Cut a piece of lining 12 inches (30 cm) by 4 inches (10 cm) and pin it to the same area, but on the right side of the fabric. Baste a straight line of thread 8 inches (20 cm) long exactly where the zipper opening is to be, basting through the lining piece at the same time. Now parallel to this basting thread, ⅛ inch (1 mm) on either side, stitch the lining piece and muff together. Then cut exactly through the middle of the resulting rectangle, cutting into the corners to the stitching at each end. Pull the lining fabric through the wrong side, pull it tight, pin to the wrong side, and sew fast by hand. Now sew in an 8-inch (20-cm)-long zipper by hand or machine. Make a pocket of sturdy cotton measuring 8 inches (20 cm) by 8¾ inches (22 cm). Sew this fast on the inside at either side of the zipper so that a little pocketbook is formed. Fold the muff over with the right sides facing [see pattern], sew together along the sides, snip into the seam edges, turn right side out, and flatten. Pin the piece of lining with the right side against the right side of the overlap and sew them together along the outside edges. Make V-notches in the seam edge curves, turn right side out, flatten, and press. Sew the lining fast to the inside by hand. Fold the muff double over once again, and sew securely at line A [see pattern]. Make a button and loop or a snap fastener closure. Sew a cord or ribbon to the muff so

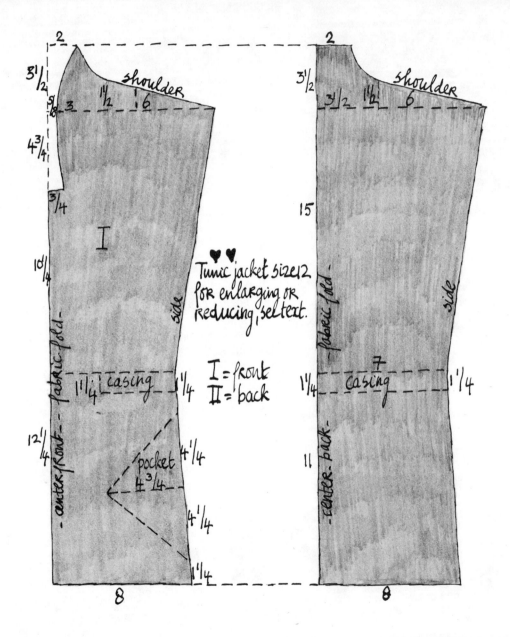

2

$3\frac{1}{2}$

$\frac{5}{8}$   3   $1\frac{1}{2}$   shoulder   6

$4\frac{3}{4}$

$\frac{3}{4}$

I

$10\frac{1}{4}$

– center front – – fabric fold –

$1\frac{1}{4}$   casing   $1\frac{1}{4}$

side

$12\frac{1}{4}$

pocket   $4\frac{1}{4}$

$4\frac{3}{4}$

$4\frac{1}{4}$

$1\frac{1}{4}$

8

♥ ♥
Tunic jacket size 12
for enlarging or
reducing, see text.

I = front
II = back

2

$3\frac{1}{2}$

$3\frac{1}{2}$   $1\frac{1}{2}$   shoulder   6

15

– fabric fold –

$1\frac{1}{4}$   casing   $1\frac{1}{4}$
7

side

11

– center back –

8

A deliciously warm tunic that can be worn over a thick sweater. You can also make it of a lighter material for indoor wear. The tunic is pulled on over the head. It has open sides that are fastened with laces sewn to the ends of a casing through which an elastic is drawn. Suitable material: a wool fabric, tweed, a heavy cotton, corduroy, padded nylon, etc.

## VARIATIONS
Make front and back of contrasting fabrics, with pockets matching the back side.

## FABRIC REQUIRED
$1\frac{1}{8}$ yards (1 m), 54 inches (135 cm) or 45 inches (115 cm) wide; or $2\frac{1}{4}$ yards (2 m), 36 inches (90 cm) wide.
**For the lining** $1\frac{1}{8}$ yards (1 m), 54 inches (135 cm) wide.

## ENLARGING OR REDUCING PATTERN
Add (enlarge) or subtract (reduce) $\frac{1}{2}$ inch ($1\frac{1}{4}$ cm) per size change at the side seams of the front and back. The waistline moves up (reducing) or down (enlarging) $\frac{1}{4}$ inch ($\frac{5}{8}$ cm) per size change, and the neckline is enlarged or reduced $\frac{1}{4}$ inch ($\frac{5}{8}$ cm) all around per size change.

## CUTTING
Lay the pattern pieces with the "fabric fold" against the folded edge of the doubled-over material. Allow $\frac{5}{8}$ inch ($1\frac{1}{2}$ cm) all around for seams. Cut out again from a lining fabric. Cut pockets out twice from both tunic and lining fabrics. For the casing at the back, cut a strip of material $16\frac{1}{2}$ inches (42 cm) by 2 inches (5 cm)—include $\frac{1}{2}$-inch ($1\frac{1}{4}$-cm) seam allowance on both sides along the length. For the casing at the front, cut two strips measuring 6 inches (15 cm) by 2 inches (5 cm). For the lacing with which the tunic is tied closed, cut four strips measuring 14 inches (35 cm) by $3\frac{1}{4}$ inches ($8\frac{1}{8}$ cm)—include $\frac{1}{2}$-inch ($1\frac{1}{4}$-cm) seam allowance along both sides.

## SEWING
Pin the lining to the front and back sections, right sides facing. Stitch fast all around except at the shoulder seams. Trim seam edges back to $\frac{3}{8}$ inch ($\frac{3}{4}$ cm), snip the corners, and make small notches in the curves. Turn right side out, flatten, and press. Now pin and sew the shoulder seams together, but don't sew the lining—leave that loose momentarily. Snip notches into the seam edge curves, and then press. Now pin the lining to the shoulder seam, rather loosely lest the lining pull, and sew down by hand with small stitches. Pin the casings on the front and back sections, where indicated, turning in at the ends, but leaving the casings open so that you can draw the elastic through. Pin and sew the fastening strips to a finished width of $1\frac{1}{4}$ inches (3 cm). For the back section, cut a piece of elastic 12 inches (30 cm) long and 1 inch ($2\frac{1}{2}$ cm) wide. Sew the fastening strips to the ends of the elastic, and then draw through the back casing. Stretch the elastic and sew securely at the ends of the casing. For the front, cut two pieces of elastic 3 inches ($7\frac{1}{2}$ cm) by 1 inch ($2\frac{1}{2}$ cm). Sew a fastening strip to one end of either elastic and then draw through the casing on the front. Stretch the elastic and sew securely at the casing ends, once on the left and once on the right. Staystitch around the entire tunic $\frac{1}{2}$ inch ($1\frac{1}{4}$ cm) from the edges.

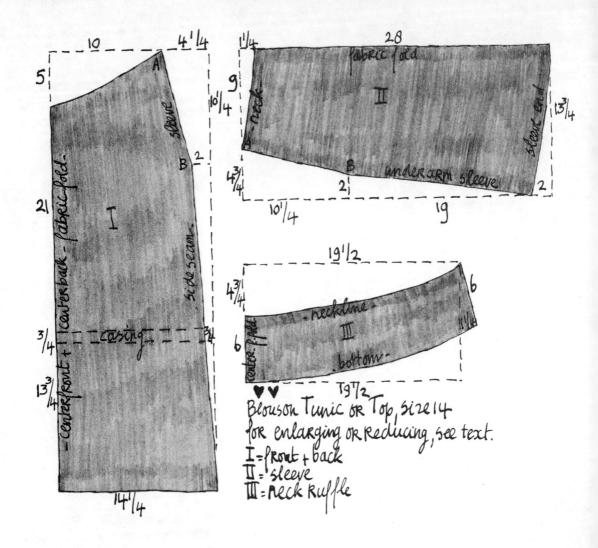

**Piece I (front + back):**

10     4'1/4

5

A

— sleeve —

B   2

I

21

— center front + center back - Fabric fold. —

— side seam —

3/4    casing    3/4

13 3/4

14'1/4

**Piece II (sleeve):**

1/4        28

Fabric fold

9

II

— neck —

sleeve end

13 3/4

4 3/4

B   underarm sleeve

2           2

10'1/4        19

10'1/4

**Piece III (neck ruffle):**

19'1/2

4 3/4               6

— neckline —

center fold

III

6             11'1/4

— bottom —

19'1/2

♥ ♥

Blouson Tunic or Top, size 14
for enlarging or reducing, see text.
I = front + back
II = sleeve
III = neck Ruffle

# BLOUSON TUNIC OR TOP

A wide, full blouson top that can be made with or without a ruffle at the neckline.

## VARIATIONS
With or without a ruffle, a casing and belt at the hips, or cut shorter and gathered onto a straight band with a button closing at the left on the hip.

## FABRIC REQUIRED
**With ruffle** $5\frac{1}{2}$ yards (5 m), 36 inches (90 cm) wide; $4\frac{7}{8}$ yards ($4\frac{1}{2}$ m), 45 inches (115 cm) wide; or $3\frac{1}{4}$ yards (3 m) 54 inches (135 cm) wide.
**Without ruffle** $4\frac{1}{2}$ yards (4 m), 36 inches (90 cm) or 45 inches (115 cm) wide; or $3\frac{1}{4}$ yards (3 m), 54 inches (135 cm) wide.

## ENLARGING OR REDUCING PATTERN
Add (enlarge) or subtract (reduce) $\frac{1}{2}$ inch ($1\frac{1}{4}$ cm) per size change at the side and underarm seams. For the ruffle, add or subtract $\frac{1}{2}$ inch ($1\frac{1}{4}$ cm) per size change at the "fabric fold."

## CUTTING
Lay the pattern pieces with the "fabric fold" against the folded edge of the doubled-over material. Cut out with a $\frac{5}{8}$-inch ($1\frac{1}{2}$-cm) seam allowance and a $2\frac{1}{2}$-inch ($6\frac{1}{4}$-cm) hem allowance at the bottom. Cut out all the pattern pieces twice from the folded material.
**Blouse gathered to a hipband** Cut off the pattern to 2 inches (5 cm) below the casing line. For the hipband, cut a strip of fabric 60 inches (150 cm) by $6\frac{1}{2}$ inches (16 cm).
**Blouse with casing** Cut a strip of fabric 56 inches (140 cm) by $1\frac{1}{2}$ inches ($3\frac{3}{4}$ cm) for the casing and a strip 70 inches (175 cm) by 2 inches (5 cm) for the belt.

## SEWING
Pin and sew points A and B of the front section to points A and B respectively of the sleeves, and then points A and B of the sleeve back to points A and B of the blouse back. (You will have an enormous neckline at this point, but it will be reduced to normal proportions by gathering in with an elastic or small cord). Press the seam edges open. Pin and sew the underarm seams and the side seams. Reinforce at the armpit with an extra line of stitching, and snip into the seam edges there. Press the seam edges open.

**Blouse without ruffle** Precisely at the center front and $\frac{5}{8}$ inch ($1\frac{1}{2}$ cm) from the edge, make a buttonhole through which a small cord can be drawn. Sew a rolled hem $\frac{5}{8}$ inch ($1\frac{1}{2}$ cm) wide and draw the cord or an elastic through that. Pull in and tie securely at the desired neck width.

**Blouse with ruffle** Determine the center of each sleeve top and mark it with a pin. This is where the ruffle for the front and the back neck begins and ends. Wrong sides together, stitch the ruffle to the blouse neckline $\frac{1}{8}$ inch (1 mm) from the edge. Run a second row of stitching around the neckline $\frac{3}{4}$ inch ($1\frac{7}{8}$ cm) from the edge. You now have a casing about $\frac{5}{8}$ inch ($1\frac{1}{2}$ cm) wide through which a cord or ribbon is drawn—to be pulled in, thus creating the ruffle—and tied at the shoulders on the right and left. Fold the ruffle strip back onto the blouse front.

**Blouse with casing** Pin and sew the casing on where indicated. Leave about 2 inches (5 cm) open at center front. Sew the belt, draw it through the casing, pull in and tie securely at center front.

**Blouse gathered to a hipband** At the bottom left front, make a $2\frac{3}{4}$-inch ($6\frac{7}{8}$-cm) opening and finish this with a piece of overlay. Gather the blouse bottom in to 40 inches (100 cm) for size 14, adjusting the gathers evenly. Pin and sew the hipband to the blouse with the right sides facing. Press the seam edges upward. Fold the hipband over double to the wrong side of the blouse and sew securely there. Finish the ends.

# ALTERATION TIPS

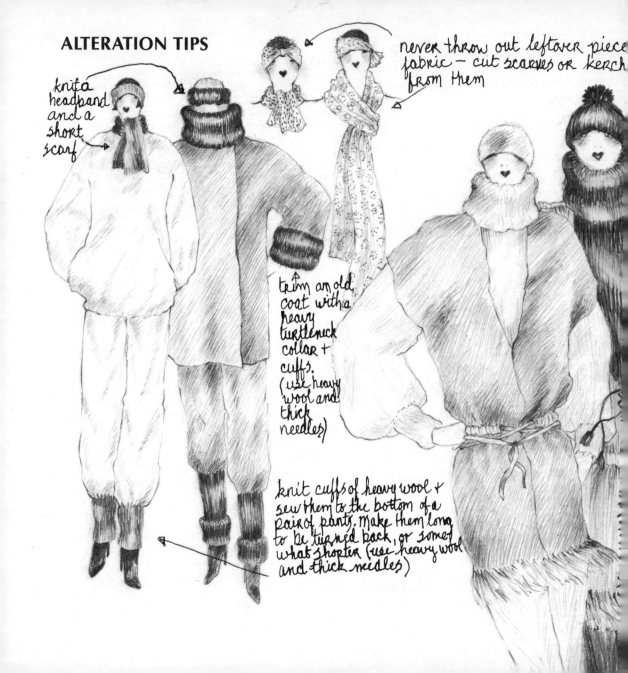

knit a headband and a short scarf

never throw out leftover pieces fabric – cut scarves or kerch from them

trim an old coat with a heavy turtleneck collar + cuffs. (use heavy wool and thick needles)

knit cuffs of heavy wool + sew them to the bottom of a pair of pants. Make them long to be turned back, or somewhat shorter (use heavy wool and thick needles)

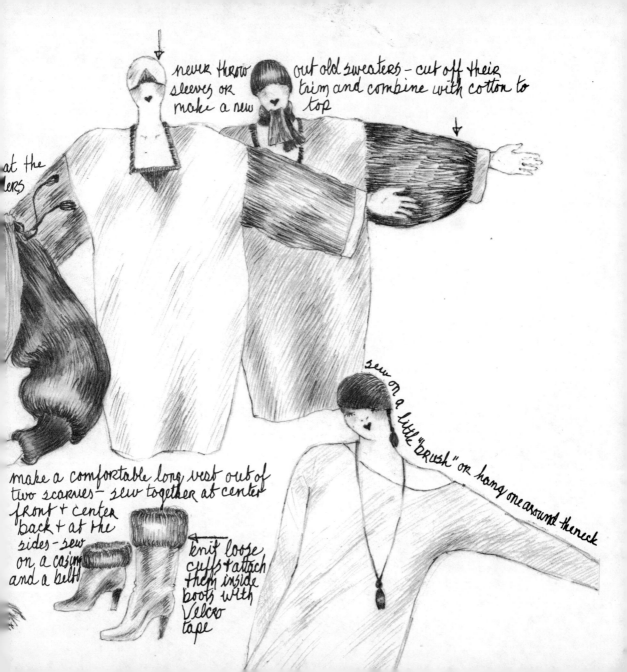

never throw out old sweaters - cut off their sleeves or trim and combine with cotton to make a new top

at the ers

sew on a little "BRUSH" or hang one around the neck

make a comfortable long vest out of two scarves - sew together at center front + center back + at the sides - sew on a casing and a belt

knit loose cuffs + attach them inside boots with Velcro tape